Pink Lemonade

A Jubilant Survivor's Story about Overcoming Life's Challenges and Emerging Triumphantly

Tamara Kaye Severin

Stay strong!
♡ *Tamara Kaye*

iUniverse®

PINK LEMONADE
A Jubilant Survivor's Story About Overcoming Life's Challenges And Emerging Triumphantly

iUniverse books may be ordered through booksellers or by contacting:

iUniverse LLC
1663 Liberty Drive
Bloomington, IN 47403
www.iuniverse.com
1-800-Authors (1-800-288-4677)

Because of the dynamic nature of the Internet, any web addresses or links contained in this book may have changed since publication and may no longer be valid. The views expressed in this work are solely those of the author and do not necessarily reflect the views of the publisher, and the publisher hereby disclaims any responsibility for them.

Any people depicted in stock imagery provided by Thinkstock are models, and such images are being used for illustrative purposes only. Certain stock imagery © Thinkstock.

ISBN: 978-1-4917-3858-0 (sc)
ISBN: 978-1-4917-3859-7 (hc)
ISBN: 978-1-4917-3860-3 (e)

Library of Congress Control Number: 2014911394

Printed in the United States of America

iUniverse rev. date: 06/23/2014

Contents

Dedication

Laura, you are the sweetest lemonade God ever made.
Many thanks to Renee for numerous hours of editing
and more than fifty-two years of dear friendship.
Ronna, you create happiness and add joy to my life.
Doctor DellaCroce, you are my knight in shining armor.
Johnny, Craig, Mom, Dad, and Tiki, thanks
for loving me unconditionally.
I would also like to recognize several other
individuals who gave me love and support:
Cathy, Claire, Chris, Deb, Linda, Peggy, Ronnie, Sandy,
Susan, Teri, my caring neighbors, my Vespa buddies,
and my County of Orange co-workers who generously
donated their hard-earned hours during my recovery.

"For the Spirit God gave us does not make us timid,
but gives us power, love and self-discipline."
(2 Timothy 1:7 NIV)

Foreword

A firsthand account of one woman's journey through breast cancer treatment and the loss of both breasts to her disease. Tammy's account of the struggle to find information on the newest technology and the amount of personal research that was required are a testament to the chasm that still exists between women and caregivers on the forefront of pioneering advances in the art of breast reconstruction. Her tenacious spirit and self-directed care choices allowed her to go against the grain and eventually find the best individual care combination. Her writing is full of sage pearls of advice for anyone facing breast cancer and the treatments that come with it. There is no more-valuable resource for a woman facing breast cancer than the voice of one who has been there before her. Essential reading for all who are affected by breast cancer.

Dr. Frank DellaCroce
Center for Restorative Breast Surgery and St. Charles Surgical Hospital
New Orleans, Louisiana

Prologue

"You look like a Coke can."

I'm stunned; did he actually just call me a Coke can? For the price I'm paying, I cannot believe the treatment I'm getting. Sitting only twelve inches across from this doctor (who looks like he spends as much time at the gym as he does in surgery), I can tell that he's completely unaware of my embarrassment over my distorted chest. Instead he is casually making derogatory comments that only make me feel more uncomfortable and embarrassed. Does he not comprehend that I'm here to have a consultation about reconstructive surgery due to my bilateral mastectomy? Does he not even understand breast cancer?

Never have I gotten dressed and fled an office building so fast. Tears flow down my cheeks as I make my way out of the building and over to my car. As I sit in my car in the parking lot, I feel so humiliated. This isn't my body. It's a body drugged, disfigured, and discarded by cancer. It's so bad that even the doctor makes fun of it.

As I shift my car into gear, I realize that I need to stop feeling sorry for myself and find an answer to this problem. God never does things randomly; He has purpose behind everything that happens to us. *Dear God, please get me out of this box that's been suffocating me for the past year; show me the answer.*

Chapter 1

TWO YEARS EARLIER

June 20, 2007

The mammogram took way longer than I expected it to. When I agreed to come in for this mammogram, I thought I would be in and out in no time at all. My ob-gyn had told me that she really thought I should get in right away since she had found an offensive lump in my right breast. Since I had already arranged for the day off to attend my son's sixth-grade graduation ceremony and luncheon, I agreed. My plan was to leave right after the ceremony and be back in time for lunch. My neighbor and friend Norma agreed to take Craig home with her and her own graduate after the ceremony, and I would meet up with them in a couple of hours. This seemed like a reasonable plan to me, since my ob-gyn was being very insistent.

I definitely didn't want to miss the graduation. After all, the main reason I had taken a job with the County of Orange when Craig started first grade was so I would not miss important events. This was certainly one of those events. When he was a baby and in kindergarten, quite often I was gone for days at a time, traveling to foreign countries to speak or conducting training that might last for days. A very conscious decision was made for me to stay close to home during his years in school so that I could be an involved parent. Therefore, I thought nothing of trying to do both.

When I first arrived at the x-ray facility, they took the standard, uncomfortable mammogram. Then the technician started getting a funny look on her face. The next thing I knew, she called in another technician, who took about seven pictures of my left breast. At that point my impatient nature reared up, and I said, "Uh, excuse me, but isn't the lump in question on the right side?"

Of course they never give anything away that might frighten the patient unnecessarily, so she said, "Oh, I just saw something on the left that I'm double-checking." Great, all I could think about was how uncomfortable I was and *Let's get this over with. I have a celebration to attend!*

Much to my surprise, I was asked to please keep my robe on and take a seat outside the x-ray room. When I asked them why, they just said that it was necessary to do another test because the mammogram wasn't giving them a clear enough picture. At this point I was not worried about my breasts; I was upset because now I would undoubtedly miss lunch! After about fifteen minutes, I was asked to step inside the dimly lit ultrasound room.

After I hopped up on the table and stretched out, a technician pulled back my gown and began to slather my breasts with warm goop. She then began to slide the wand all over each breast. She was digging the wand in, and it was not a pleasant experience. The last time I had an ultrasound was when I was thirty-four years old and pregnant with Craig. Now, eleven years later, it was not such a positive experience. The whole time she was dragging the wand around my chest, she had a funny look on her face. The way the table was angled, I couldn't see the screen. Before I could ask her what was going on, she did the same thing as the mammogram gal; she had another technician come in and do all the same ultrasounds all over again. The second technician dug the wand in much deeper and more painfully and was still not saying anything. Because the table was positioned so that I was unable to see the screen, the only thing I could do was look at her face in the glow of the screen and try to make out what was going on. But she was good at hiding it, so I got nothing. When I asked her what she thought, she just told me to sit tight and she'd be right back. That was the first time I really started to think that there might be something wrong. I felt my stomach do a summersault. So frustrating! She finally brought in the radiologist to look at the screen. I was surprised to see her enter the room; they usually decipher it and get back to the patient later. Again I felt those summersaults.

Well, not only did the radiologist look at the screen, but she said that I would need to have a biopsy done. What? No time for me to think, prepare, or even react. Before I could even comment, the nurse was swabbing me and prepping me. No one asked me if I had someone waiting in the lobby or if I had other plans. *Hey, what about my lunch?* The radiologist whipped out this huge "gun" with a six-inch needle. At that point she told me she was going to take twelve biopsies! Yikes! I hate needles, and this was the biggest needle I'd seen in a long time. And it was pointed at me. The first thing she did was give me twelve shots of lidocaine with another needle that just happened to be waiting in the wings. Then with the gun she took twelve core samples of my breast tissue. It felt like when you get your ears pierced and the gun snaps *ga-gunk*. It's an uncomfortable experience to say the least. All this, and I was still not wrapping my head around *why* they felt that all this was necessary. The *C* word was never mentioned, and when I asked if this was routine, I was told that it was "recommended" since I was already there. Most of the women I know love to share information, especially if it's health related. Not these women; I was getting nothing from them.

The next thing I knew, I was packed in ice and being told to go home and take it easy, perhaps with some Tylenol to help with the pain. When I walked out, I was surprised to see my husband sitting in the waiting room. I had no idea he would come down to the medical center. I was thinking that he would have left his shop and gone straight home, ready to celebrate Craig's graduation. He looked up as I trudged over to him, my blouse stretched tight against the extra weight and volume of the ice packs underneath, and said, "You've been gone for hours! I was starting to get worried. You didn't answer your phone, and Craig said you didn't show up for the luncheon either."

I told him that I wasn't expecting to be gone all day and now that I had missed everything, I was really upset. At this point I was keenly aware of what the outcome of all these tests might be. Not wanting to further throw a damper on things or get him alarmed prematurely, I said nothing about the procedures other than how long they took. Not being a guy who wants to know too much about female issues, Johnny didn't ask. That was something I would need to keep in mind over the next few days, weeks, months, and even years.

Not being able to muster the energy needed to go out to dinner with five pounds of ice packed into my already full 36 DDD bra, I stayed home and sulked. More importantly, I avoided the celebration so as to not embarrass Craig on his special day. It was just one of the many times yet to come that cancer would interfere with my plans.

The next day at my office, I mentioned this ordeal to a couple of friends. Their eyes got big, and they were immediately alarmed. One particular sensitive and caring friend started to cry and reach out to hug me. As I gave her a big hug (and reassured her), I told them both that I had no intention of getting worked up over something until I had reason to do so. Goodness, I had more important things to worry about than what "might" happen. I reminded them that I now had a twelve-year-old out of school for the summer, a new position at one of the other agencies that I had to prepare for, and a whole office to pack up. As they slipped past the stacks of boxes in my office, I waved my hands toward the partially packed boxes and said, "There are more pressing issues that I need to focus on, but I promise to keep you posted." I could see the skepticism in their faces, but they agreed that I was right. In my mind breast cancer was low on the priority list. I had no family history, I was healthy, and I had never smoked. The thought of me having cancer was a ridiculous thought to me at that point and was not worth wasting my energy on. Besides, it was already Friday, and I had to be packed and out of my office by the following week, ready to start in my new position. Priorities.

The weekend came and went without any mention of the test or what the biopsies might reveal. I didn't bring it up, and of course, neither did Johnny. No phone call on Monday, but on Tuesday afternoon as I walked through the front door at home, the phone was ringing. I had been thrown a good-bye party by my coworkers, all wishing me well since I would be gone in a few days, off to share my talent with one of the other agencies at the County of Orange. As I walked over to answer the phone, I was thinking that it might be someone who hadn't been able to make it to my good-bye party but wanted to speak to me before my last day.

"Tamara? Is this Tamara Severin?" Obviously this caller was not one of my friends as I had thought. Perhaps a telemarketer; I was in too good of a mood to even be bothered by that. Suddenly I was jolted to attention. What did she just say? She was telling me that the results were in and I needed to make an appointment to come see the doctor.

I told her, "Anything you have to tell me can be said over the phone." Her words made no sense to me. Why did I need to drive all the way back over to the doctor's office to speak to a doctor I've only met once, if in fact it was even the same doctor as the one who did the biopsies? I told her as much, and she repeated that I would need to make an appointment.

At that point I started to get upset. My head started to put it all together, and I was reacting not only to what she was saying but to what she was *not* saying. Rather abruptly I said, "If you have information that I need, I suggest you find someone who can communicate that to me over the phone, because I will not be coming back into your office," and I hung up.

Within five minutes the phone rang again. I answered, "Hello," and a different female voice on the other end of the line said, "Tamara, Tamara Severin?"

I answered, "Yes, how can I help you?"

This woman said, "I understand you do not want to come in and get your results for the biopsies that were performed last week." Once again I explained that I would like the results to be given to me over the phone just as I had requested when I was at the office the day the tests were performed. Nothing had changed. I had told the doctor the previous week that I did not want to have to come back in, and I hadn't changed my mind. Unaffected, she told me that she didn't have the authority to give me the results over the phone and so it would be necessary for me to set up an appointment. By that time, I had heard enough, and I said, "When you have someone who has the authority, please have them give me a call. If I don't hear back from anyone, I will assume the results came back fine," and once again I hung up the phone.

About fifteen minutes later Johnny got home from work and asked me how my day was. Just as I began to tell him about the going-away party that had been given in my honor, the phone rang again. Seeing me reach to get it, he turned and went in to the living room to say hello to our little Yorkie and turn on the TV to watch the evening news. This time when I answered the phone, I was prepared and was actually in a calmer frame of mind than I had been in for the previous two calls. The voice on the other end of the line was a completely new voice to me, and I listened as she explained that the other two nurses were only following protocol and were not allowed to deliver any information to patients, and she said that she hoped I would understand.

I said, "Yes, I can understand that, but I did leave instructions for the information to be given to me over the phone, and that's why I was getting upset with them."

She assured me that she would now give me the results and I would not have to drive back over to the office. As I reached for a piece of paper and pen, she blurted out, "You have cancer (long pause), in both breasts."

Chapter 2

SPARKLERS OR SECRETS

July 2, 2007

It was the first day of summer school for Craig. He hated having to go, and I hated fighting with him over it. Just because I had been diagnosed with cancer didn't mean that the rest of my life was on hold. It was just the opposite; my life was in full swing. I was ready to move into my new position as the training manager at the Auditor-Controller's office, and my annual Fourth of July party was right around the corner. I realized that this was quite a bit to be thinking about given the news that I had just received. But I also hoped that it would keep my mind from dwelling on the cancer all day. To add to the stress, I hadn't been sleeping well at night, tossing, turning, and burning up all night long. Several times over the weekend I had gotten up in the middle of the night frantic for answers. I would slide out of bed quietly and spend the next several hours in the kitchen on line looking at everything I could find regarding breast cancer. It was overwhelming. The scars on the women bold enough to post them were horrifying. And the reconstructions were sadly not really worth calling reconstructions; more like hack jobs. Not having talked to a plastic surgeon yet, I didn't know what to expect, and the Internet provided my only insight.

There was still so much to do: decorations, food items to be made (I learned long ago never to never rely on someone else to provide main entrees), and the planning of beverages. It had been so hot that I made a mental note to include some type of frozen treat for the dessert. After work I went to the craft store to get some decorations. While I was standing in line to pay, I started to feel weird, like I might faint. That was very unusual for me. By the time I got up to the counter, I was ready to go down. Because I was so embarrassed by the whole thing, I quickly paid and went directly out to my Vespa. By the time I got outside, things were going gray. I tried to sit on the curb and get my head down. Things were buzzing in my ears and I thankfully managed to remain conscious, but I was in no condition to drive a scooter home. After my head stopped spinning, I threw up in the bushes a few times. *What is going on?* Finally I felt calm enough to hop on the scooter and head home. I won't lie; it was a very shaky ride home, one I probably shouldn't have attempted. When I told Johnny about it later, he glared at me and said, "What's wrong with you? Why didn't you call me? I would have come and picked you up!"

I started to cry and said, "I don't know. I didn't want to bother you. I never know if you are out on a job site or have a customer in your shop. For all I know you would have been in the back of your shop welding and not even heard the phone ringing."

I stopped talking and blew my nose. I realized that what I was saying sounded stupid, but I just wasn't thinking. I was so used to taking care of myself that I just thought I could continue doing so. I was an only child, and my parents raised me to be extremely self-sufficient. They were so afraid I would be a "spoiled only child" that they may have gone too far in the other direction. From the time I was an adolescent, I was encouraged to get part-time jobs and learn to do things that most kids my age weren't doing. Naturally, I had chores too, but they weren't the typical chores that most little girls do. In addition to keeping my room clean, I had to go outside and pick up our little dog's "mess." As I got older I was taught by my dad how to mow the yard and skim and vacuum our built-in swimming pool. I still remember scooping leaves and frogs out of the pool when I was a teenager. My first real job was when I was twelve years old. I worked at 7-Eleven from 3:00 till 5:00 stocking the shelves and changing prices on cans of tuna and green beans. The old-fashioned price "gun" that slapped on tiny paper price tags was nestled in my red and white store apron along with a box cutter. I was armed and dangerous (if you were a case of toilet paper), and I was earning a whopping $1.00 an hour, so I meant business. After school I would ride my bicycle two blocks to the 7-Eleven on the corner and report for work at least three days a week. In addition to my duties as a stock person, I was often called upon to pour Slurpees. Cherry or Cola, that was the only choice, and the customer never poured their own! This was the greatest thrill for me, especially when kids that I knew from the neighborhood would come in to get a Slurpee and see me. Naturally, I was the envy of many in those days. From a very early age, I was told by my parents, "You can do it. Don't *get scared*; just *get going*." So I suppose it was just my natural instinct to assume that I could do it all myself. But I would soon learn that that's not the way to beat cancer.

After I calmed down, Johnny put his arms around me and told me it was going to be all right. Then I could tell he wanted to ask me something, so I said, "What? Do you think you know what is wrong with me?"

He said, "No, but I am wondering if it has something to do with the cancer."

I said, "I can't imagine it would. I'm not on any kind of medication yet, and I only just learned about the cancer myself, so I don't think it's related." Disregarding my discomfort, I once again began to feel the pressure of getting things done, and I said, "I just wish I felt better, because you know we have ten people coming over for the Fourth and I have so much to do."

After I said that he still stood there looking at me, so I said, "What?"

"Well, uh, how do you want to handle this? I mean, do you want to keep it to ourselves, or are you going to tell anyone?"

I gazed back at him, stunned. How could he ask that? Decisively I said, "Well, I don't think I'll be able to hide it." My husband had lost his mother to lymphoma a few years before, and I knew that this was influencing the way he was reacting to my situation now. He agreed to support me in whatever decision I made or in any way I wanted to handle my illness; I told him that there should be no secrets from our family and friends.

Although it had never occurred to me to keep it a secret, his words did get me to thinking about how I planned on telling people. After telling Johnny what my phone caller had revealed, I told my son Craig that I had received news from the doctor that meant I had to have some more tests and that he shouldn't worry. Whatever they discovered would be dealt with. I knew I didn't have to give him all of the details at that point, but he was smart enough to know something was going on when suddenly I started going to doctor visits and making numerous phone calls. As time went by, I would be able to fill him in on information; as much as his twelve-year-old brain could handle. Besides, he was more concerned with fitting in at his new middle school and dealing with his summer school class than he was with his mom. He was well into his "tween" stage, and the more distance he had from the "parental units" the better, in his mind.

After talking with Craig, I took the phone out on to our patio to call my parents. Of course they were shattered when I told them. I'll never forget my mom saying with a cry in her voice, "Oh no!" In that conversation I wound up doing most of the reassuring and convincing them that it would all be okay, even if I didn't have any guarantees at that point. My coworkers would have to wait to be told; I was leaving soon, and that was not the way I wanted to be remembered.

As it turned out, someone stuck their head in my office as I was tearfully packing one of my last boxes of training materials. She said, "I'm sorry. Did I catch you at a bad time?"

I told her, "No, I'm okay, just realizing what a pack rat I have become since moving in to this office."

She replied, "Oh, it looks like you've been crying. Are you sure everything is all right?"

I wiped my eyes, looked down into the box I was working on, and said, "Yes, I'm fine. I'm just going to miss everyone."

She smiled and told me how much they would miss me and left me to my packing. As she walked away I felt horrible about lying to her, but I just couldn't bear to be leaving with that at my legacy. No, I would tell people but on my terms. I realized that there are some things you tell your family and friends, while other people get a little less information, and then some are on a need-to-know basis. At this point, she didn't need to know.

That night was spent doing as much research as I could. I was clueless about what to expect, as cancer had never been on my radar before. By 2:00 the next morning, I had completed an e-mail to my best friends. As I hit the *send* button, I thought, *Let the game begin*. Only this time, it really wasn't a game. Several of those friends would be coming over on the Fourth of July, and I certainly didn't want to spend the evening discussing cancer. Nope, my party would not be ruined. I already had ideas for red, white, and blue desserts, and time was running out.

Chapter 3

A DIFFICULT LETTER TO WRITE

Dear Friends,   *July 3, 2007*

As most of you know, I have been offered a new promotion. My start date is July 6. In preparation for that, I have been getting things done, vet appointments, dentists, and ob-gyn. As a result of the latter, my ob-gyn found a lump in my right breast.

She sent me in for a mammogram/ultrasound the next week. They were all in a dither and did two rounds of everything. The next thing you know, I was having twelve biopsies! (Stay with me.)

I got the results two nights ago, unfortunately, not good. They found cancer in both *breasts. Stage one and two. Good grief! Talk about* bad *timing. Don't they know I have a new fabulous job to start????*

I just got back from the breast surgeon tonight, and we (me and my breasts) are going in for a double mastectomy in about three weeks. He said it was one of the most unusual cases he's ever seen, and I had the radiology team in a total uproar because they've never seen two lumps in the same exact spot in each breast.

My surgeon said because they were close to the lymph nodes (almost under my arms) he really thought taking it all out (rather than a lumpectomy) was the best way to save my life.

I may still have to have chemo depending on what they find, and I'll be out of work for about a month. That bugs me. I hate knowing I am starting a new job and then leaving for a month.

So, I want you to know I've already told my mom and rather than have this conversation seven more times, I hope you don't mind the e-mail. I didn't want this to come up years from now and you say, "Why didn't you tell me?" And I DO plan on being around in years from now to talk about it!

I'll take any and all prayers you want to send up for me, and I know I have your love and support. I'm so lucky to have such dear friends as you.

Johnny is fine, already telling me I'll be a real *Orange County girl when it's all over. At first he was freaked (we all were) as you know his mother died of lymphatic cancer, so he imagined the worst. Now that we've been to the surgeon, heard the whole story, and have a plan of action, he's much calmer.*

Feel free to call. I'm fine with talking about it. I just wanted to tell you all as soon as I could and this was the easiest way to do that.
–Tam

It was surprising to see how people responded to this kind of news. Some people didn't call or write to me for almost a year. They would tell me later that they didn't know what to say to me. That's probably true; some people don't know what to say or do in tough situations. As I think back on those "friends," I realize that they are the ones who have perhaps needed to be cared for themselves and are not really the strongest; therefore I didn't hold it against them. Others called me all the time, went out of their way to make sure I knew they were thinking about me, and stopped by to see me. In fact some people that I wasn't even that close to but knew of my illness sent lovely cards, care packages, and hand-knitted scarves. I was overwhelmed by the generosity and compassion of those thoughtful people.

One of the most powerful e-mails I received right after sending out the letter was from my friend in Oregon. He and his wife Ronna had been dear friends ever since we lived next door to each other in Huntington Beach back in the eighties. He simply wrote, "This sucks." Well said, Mike, well said.

Chapter 4

MY WEIRD VIRUS/RASH/BLOOD CLOT AND, OH YEAH, CANCER

July 4, 2007

Not the way I envisioned spending my Fourth of July: red and hot all over! I could not get rid of the hot, itchy rash that was starting to consume my whole body. I felt like I had ants all over my hands, arms, torso, and the tops of my legs. My face was red and splotchy too. Our neighbors and friends came over with treats, decorations, and flowers. We had so much fun eating and then walked over to the park to see the fireworks. It was a great diversion for me, and I would have felt great if it weren't for the rash and itchiness going on. No one asked me anything about the cancer till the very end of the evening. They were concerned but knew that I didn't want to spoil the party; they knew that I do love hosting a good party.

July 5, 2007

I took the day off so I could meet with my oncologist. Before we could even discuss the cancer, I had to tell him about how awful I'd been feeling. I told him about the rash, fever, and slight cough I was starting to get. He discussed a bit about cancer and then sent me over for x-rays and blood work. He was very concerned about how I looked and felt. Initially he prescribed Prednisone for the rash and Cipro for the cough. Later, I got the diagnoses of a *viral* infection and discontinued the Cipro. I continued the Prednisone for five days. I hadn't even started with the cancer treatments, and already I was on steroids!

Did I brag about being a strong woman recently? Did I open my mouth about needing some action in my life? At this point I can't remember, but I have to say, "Note to self: shut up!"

July 6, 2007

First day at my new job! Since the building was a little farther down the freeway than my old office, I decided to take my car and not ride my Vespa. It was also difficult to take much on my Vespa, so I needed the extra space of my car. It turned out that I spent most of the day getting fingerprinted and having a new photo ID made. What a way to start a new job—coughing, achy, and bright red and splotchy all over; not looking good for the new ID. The photo on that badge would be a reminder of that day for years to come. If it weren't my first day, I would have called in sick and gone to see a doctor. However, I felt it just wasn't an option on that day.

Everyone was very kind, and I hoped that they would forget what a mess I was on my first day. I felt nervous because I certainly was not at my best. I felt scared that my new boss would think that she'd made a big mistake. It's hard to say if I would have felt this nervous in my normal condition, but that wasn't the situation.

My new boss spent some time with me and assured me that I was okay, and she confided in me that she was worried that I wouldn't want the job. And here I was so worried she would reject me that I didn't think about what she might have been thinking.

I was worn out that night—the viral infection was taking its toll on me. I was really looking forward to getting some sleep, because for the past week I hadn't been sleeping very well. As a matter of fact, I would have slept in that Saturday morning, but my friend Connie worked for a very well-known clothing retailer that was having their annual warehouse sale. And I was one of the two people she was allowed to invite. After looking forward to this all year, I was determined to be there, and no later than 7:00 a.m.! It would take more than a rash, a cough, or uh, cancer to keep me from a clearance sale!

July 7, 2007

Even though I was tired and itchy, I still made it to the warehouse sale by 7:00 a.m. As I waited outside the building in the long line to get in, the staff came down and distributed giant clear bags. We were to use these bags to hold the items we wished to purchase. There were no shopping carts, and most people had come to do some serious shopping. Taking the large plastic bag, I could already feel my skin starting to heat up and I felt faint. Yikes, I hadn't even entered the building yet!

The doors opened, and we flooded in as if we were starving cattle and couldn't wait to get to the troughs. People were running everywhere, and already there were bags being filled and strewn about. Abandoning their half-filled bags, discount divas (now unencumbered), scrambled off to adjacent aisles lest they miss out on a treasured two-dollar purse. It was one of the abandoned bags spilling its contents of socks, headbands, and costume jewelry into my path that made it crystal clear that it was time for me to leave. As I rounded the end of the aisle in my heated haze, my foot caught on it and I sprawled across the end of the display of leg warmers. It had been less than thirty minutes since I had been in the building, but now it was clear that I must abandon this sinking ship. I trudged up to the counter. The workers behind it looked at me, and one cashier said, "Are you sure you are ready to cash out? You just got here, and there are lots more good deals to be had today." I didn't say a word. I just handed her a five-dollar bill and slung my barely used clear plastic bag over my shoulder and walked out.

Driving home, I thought to myself, *I should have just driven my scooter, I bought so little today.* My plan was to really stock up on the amazing deals and treasures, so I had taken my car. As it turned out, it was a good thing, because on the way home I started to get very ill and realized that I might not make it, so I drove to the first urgent care I saw. I dragged myself up to the counter and explained my symptoms, and they took me right in. The doctor who saw me wasn't really sure what my problem was, so he did some blood work and gave me an IV of Benadryl. That worked for about two hours, but by the time I got home I started to feel miserable again.

After lying around the house most of the day, I was still lying awake at 11:00 p.m. wracking my brain over what could be going on with me. Every doctor asked me the same question: "What's different? What have you changed in your routine lately?" That was the big question, wasn't it? The short answer … everything! Actually I hadn't changed much, even though my life had changed around me. I'd really been considering this question, and the only thing I could think of was the fact that I had recently had a very heavy period. This had happened because I was told to stop taking the birth control pills immediately. The surgeon told me that my tumors were hormone receptive and birth control pills are chock full of hormones that were just feeding the tumors. About two weeks after stopping them I started having a pretty heavy flow and needed to use super absorbent tampons; something I had never needed to do before. It occurred to me to read the insert from the box to see if there were side effects; perhaps that's what I was experiencing. The insert talked about the symptoms of toxic shock. As I read about the side effects, I was mortified; I realized that I had most of the symptoms—fever, rash, cough—and the leaflet said that if you have a fever along with these symptoms get to an emergency room immediately. I leaped out of bed and ran down the hall to where Johnny was lying on the couch watching TV and said, "Johnny, listen to what this pamphlet says (I read the whole thing to him). I think we need to go to the ER right now!"

The ER staff couldn't find anything wrong with me, said I most definitely did not have toxic shock, and sent me home, stating that I could take some Benadryl. Although I was exhausted by the time I got back to bed, I still didn't sleep very well. When I woke up the next morning I felt a strange sensation in my inner right arm. It is as if my arm was burned, and I could hardly stand for it to touch my side. Just what I needed; something else to be concerned over. *Lord,* I prayed, *I'm afraid I can't handle too many more things! I've got a son getting ready to enter middle school and a new job to focus on. Please guide me.*

July 11, 2007

Two days later my arm was so tender that I was walking around holding it up as if it was in an invisible sling. It hurt, and my fingers were numb on my right hand. I had a hard time driving my scooter home from work due to the numbness in my right hand.

Additionally, my husband left for Seattle to go attend the National Vespa Rally, Amerivespa. We had been planning to attend together. He and his friend Nyle, my friend Connie's husband, had been building a vintage Vespa with a matching trailer and entered in a contest. He asked me about going. "Are you sure you don't want to just go up for a day or two? You could fly, and Nyle and I can pick you up at the airport."

As much as I had looked forward to this trip, I told him, "No, I think this is something you should definitely do, but given how lousy I feel, I think I'd better pass." Once my arm started throbbing, I was relieved that I had made that decision but was rethinking whether he should have gone.

July 12, 2007

The next morning after I got Craig out the door to summer school I drove myself to the urgent care. When I arrived at the urgent care, the front desk receptionist looked at me and said, "Oh, you're back." I wondered if they thought I was a hypochondriac. Contrarily, the doctor on call seemed sympathetic and very concerned about my sore arm and numb fingers. As a result, he sent me straight to the hospital for an ultrasound. As luck would have it, Johnny was already on his way to Seattle. As much as I would have loved to call 911 and have a team of handsome men rescue me, I decided to drive myself. Having always been a take-charge kind of gal, I saw this as no different than any other situation that I would just naturally take care of. Later I would be admonished for that decision, but at the time just seemed like the right thing to do.

Because I used the "C" word upon admission and the urgent care doctor had called it in ahead of time, I was whisked in with very little waiting. The technician took a few ultrasound swipes and then said, "Well, it's not in your head. You must really be in pain, because you have a good-sized blood clot in your right arm."

They admitted me to the hospital right there and then.

Realizing that I wouldn't make it in to work, I called the one person I knew who would help me: Laura. Laura is my "go-to" friend. She is Florence Nightingale and Martha Stewart all rolled into one lovable friend. God has blessed Laura with the patience of a saint along with a good measure of humor. Had I known this trip to the ER was going to end with me being hospitalized, I would have called her sooner. Knowing that she was at work, I didn't want to bother her, but I knew that I could still count on her to call the right people and alert them for me. She had the phone numbers of everyone in the County as well as my friends and family. Unfortunately she wasn't at her desk when I called, so I left a message.

I then called Johnny and let him know that I was being admitted to the hospital. He was already halfway to Seattle and didn't know what to do. He said, "What? I will turn around right now and come home!" I assured him that there wasn't much he could do and I didn't think I needed him since I would be under the doctor's care from then on anyway. Looking back on it, I see that God's hand was in all of that. There was a reason my husband wasn't there with me, and I know now that it was the calm before the storm.

Johnny called my parents, and they rushed up from San Diego to be with Craig when he came home from summer school. Laura eventually got the message and started making calls for me and then drove over to the hospital, where she came rushing in to see about me. When Laura and my parents got there, I was still in the ER waiting to be admitted. They had given me some pain medicine and had put packs on my arm to get the swelling to go down. My whole upper arm was bright red. On top of that I still had the rash and fever. I was a hot mess! Thankfully, there was now someone monitoring the viral infection and giving me something for the ever-intensifying cough.

It was evening by the time I was actually admitted, and I hadn't eaten since the night before. I was starting to get a really bad headache and got a bit snippy with everyone. Another friend, Bill, who had rushed to the hospital as soon as Laura contacted him, said, "She's okay. She's sounding like her old self." Leave it to good friends to tell it like it is.

Thank God there are only twenty-four hours in a day and Thursday finally ended. Friday I started to feel better. I was introduced to Lovenox, the injections I would have to do twice a day until the day of my surgery. Normally with a blood clot the prescribed medicine is in pill form, Warfarin or Coumadin, basically rat poisoning! Given the circumstances, I had to have an injection that would leave my system within twelve hours. That way I could be ready for surgery within a day's notice. The other medications take several days to evacuate your blood stream. I couldn't believe this was happening! A shot in the stomach twice a day, and I hate shots! The nurse insisted that I try to give the injections to myself, but I was too shaky, and I almost pulled the needle out before I could plunge the medicine. The nurse made it very clear that unless I had someone to administer the shots for me, I could not leave the hospital. Thank God for Laura. She immediately volunteered to administer the shots until Johnny returned from Seattle in a few days and could take over. Although Laura was not a nurse, she was the next best thing. Unfortunately, the medicine was extremely painful going in, and it burned for about ten minutes after it entered my body. I later learned that the medicine should have been warmed up to lessen the burning effect. Also, drying the alcohol area before sticking in the needle will lessen the pain.

I was released on Friday night, and Laura took me home. She was so wonderful. She drove my car home and went back later to get her own car. What would I have done and where would I have been without her? During this time I had been talking back and forth with Johnny, and he was worried sick about what was going on and the fact that he was not there. He planned to be back by Tuesday night. In the meantime Laura was running up and down the road to her own home thirty minutes away to be with me and give me these hateful yet lifesaving injections. How blessed I was to have her in my life.

Chapter 5

DAY FROM YOU-KNOW-WHERE

July 16, 2007

Because of the blood clot, I had to have a blood test every day. I have always hated needles. When I was a child, I would begin to whimper if the nurse came in with so much as a thermometer in her hand to take my temperature. It all stemmed from an experience I had when I was about three years old. My mom tells me that people rarely remember things from when they were three, but I remember that day as if it were yesterday. My mom had taken me in to see the doctor for something, and I was required to have a shot. For whatever reason, the nurse that day had me lie on my stomach on the exam table, and she pulled down my panties. Then she said, "Okay, missy, I'm going to start to count, and when I get to the number ten you are going to get the shot." I remember not liking the way that sounded, but there was nothing I could do. My mom was seated on the other side of the room in a chair, and I remember giving her a frightened look, but she was no help. It was 1964, and in those days no one ever questioned the doctor or their nurses for that matter.

As I was giving my mom beseeching looks, the nurse began to "count," and with each number she would prick my tiny buttock. She moved the needle to a new location with each number, and finally by the time she reached the number ten she plunged the needle deep into my small body. By then I was shrieking, my mom was yelling, and nurse was threatening me with another shot if I didn't calm down. For the next hour I was inconsolable. It was a horrific experience that to this day still sends a shudder through my body when I think of it. Years later my mom told me that the nurse was fired a short time after that for incompetence. She had been there over fifty years, and although she was a wonderful nurse for most of those years, her time had come. Unfortunately, her time didn't come soon enough to suit me.

Because of my history with needles, I was not looking forward to any of the blood draws, chemo, or IVs that I knew were awaiting me. Additionally, that morning was already looking to be especially grueling for me due to a very early appointment with the plastic surgeon. It seemed that once my diagnosis was confirmed, there was a series of appointments scheduled with any doctor or surgeon who may be involved in the treatment plan. Needless to say, I went.

At 7:20 I arrived for my appointment to see the plastic surgeon. Before I was allowed to meet with her, I had to watch a full video on the two reconstruction procedures available to me. The first procedure presented on the video was the breast expander and implant. This procedure is usually done at the time of the mastectomy, thus leaving the woman with a "new" breast where the removed cancerous breast (in my case breasts), had been. According to the literature, this is less "scarring" to a woman and is more convenient, as it is all done at once. That part of the video was very brief. The rest of the video was devoted to the "flap" procedure. This is where the surgeon takes your own tissue from the belly area and basically gives you a "tummy tuck" while taking the fat (while still connected to your blood supply), and tunneling it up to the breast area and forming a new breast with it. If the patient doesn't have enough fat from that area to create a new breast (or in my case two new breasts), the latissimi dorsi muscles in your back can be "filleted" and tunneled forward and be used in much the same way. This procedure is very long at ten to twelve hours and leaves two long scars down the patient's back. All this, and it takes about two months of recovery time.

After watching the full video, I was not impressed with either option, but I was open to a frank discussion with the plastic surgeon. I was completely ready to meet her. Not too long after I finished watching the video she came into the room. She seemed pleasant and professional although uncertain about what to say to me. I was about to ask her what she suggested for me when she rather abruptly said, "Well, you and I will have to discuss this at some other time. I can't perform any procedure on you because you are being treated for a blood clot, and I can't have you on the table for that long—you'll bleed to death." She told me to contact her a year later, and then she turned and walked out of the room.

Needless to say, it was blow I was not expecting. Just like that, I had no choices; the blood clot had taken them all away. Here I had been accepting the whole double mastectomy thing because I knew that I could have reconstruction and hopefully come out the other side looking even better than before. Heck, a free boob job, and all I had to do was turn in my old ones! Now what was I going to do?

Glancing at the clock, I realized that I needed to get over to the phlebotomist for my daily blood draw. I really was in no mood, not to mention that I hadn't eaten or even had anything to drink since dinner the night before. A treacherous combination, I was soon to find out.

Dehydration left my veins practically vestigial, and the phlebotomist couldn't find one to use for the blood draw. She tried to take it from my left wrist, but the needle was "rolling" around in my wrist, inflicting major pain. I started to cry and tell her it was hurting too much. She looked uncomfortable and called in another "vampire" who was waiting in the wings. This woman started on top of my hand, and after three more sticks with the needle she gave up and moved to another spot on my wrist. This was just hurting more and I started to really melt, tears rolling down my cheeks.

The final straw was when she said, "Almost done," and I said, "But I see another vial there." She casually said, "No, that's for someone else." I snapped. What did she think I was, stupid? I was forty-five years old. I wanted to say, "Don't patronize me!" I was livid.

Unbelievably, she and her cronies chimed in, saying to me, "Don't worry. You'll be fine. Lots of women go through this. No need to cry. Why are you crying? " And then the final verbal blow: "Looks like you have plenty to spare anyway."

I shot back at them, "You don't know what I have just been through. And for your information I am crying because you are *hurting* me!" Enraged, I hurried out of the building.

July 19, 2007

Because of the blood clot, necessary daily blood draws, and the impending surgery, my new boss decided that it would be better for me to be out until after the surgery and full recovery. She told me that she would take care of everything and not to worry—I would still have a job there. To think, I had only been there four days!

She put out a request to my fellow County employees for a donation of hours. This is done when an employee has a catastrophe and doesn't have enough time in their own personal bucket of accrued hours. Additionally, my former boss wrote a note of explanation to my friends at my former agency telling them about the circumstances, lest they think I had been in an accident on my Vespa! How many times had people stopped me in the hall and asked me if I was scared riding that motorcycle around all the time? I always laughed and told them, "No, that's why my husband had it custom painted Barbie-doll pink—you can't miss me! Don't worry, I've been riding for several years, and I'm always careful." In my mind I thought that is what they would think. No one would ever think I had cancer; I had not even really accepted it yet. It was such a blessing to know that I didn't have to worry where the money was coming from to pay for my health insurance. Once again, God was looking out for my well-being.

Johnny returned from Seattle and quickly learned to administer the injections to me at 7:30 in the morning and again at 7:30 at night. He always said, "I'm sorry," right before he injected me. I hated those shots, but I was thankful to have a husband with a steady hand and the nerve to do what was necessary. I have talked to so many women who admit that they or their husband would probably not be able to do it. When I ask them what they would do, they say, "Hire a nurse"! I don't think they realize the cost involved in a major illness.

I continued with the daily blood draws, and they became easier for me due to a different phlebotomist as well as my own consumption of large amounts of water before arriving for the "stick." My new wonderful phlebotomist used a gel heat pad to "bring the veins up" as well as a "baby" or what they call a "butterfly" needle. Although I already knew to ask about using that size needle, when I had asked the previous vampires to use a smaller needle, they responded with "you are having too many vials drawn; it would take too long." Ironically, my new guy had a wife undergoing breast cancer at the same time and was well aware of the trauma involved. He told me to make sure to drink plenty of water to get as hydrated as possible before coming in. He was my new hero, and I made sure to always request him for any blood draws I was required to have.

July 22, 2007

My dear friends Mike and Ronna continued to keep in touch with me and ask if there was anything they could do. Ronna had always been the kind of friend who would surprise me, the kind of person who is creative, spontaneous, and determined to make things happen once she makes her mind up. Since they left Huntington Beach and moved to Portland, I missed them often, and during this challenging time I especially craved their friendship. Ronna must have been reading my thoughts, because that sweet girl hopped in her car and drove down from Portland, Oregon! Not only did she drive over a thousand miles, but she had car trouble and almost ran off the road when her engine seized up on one of the mountain roads! God was watching out for her though. She told me later that she just kept praying for, as the song says "Jesus, take the wheel." She and I used to attend church together twenty years earlier when she lived next door to me in Huntington Beach. So that first Sunday after she arrived I was overwhelmed with joy to be worshiping in the church I love while standing next to my dear friend whom I love who had just driven so many miles out of love for me.

That same weekend my college roommate drove over three hours to see me. Although I had heard from her after she received my initial e-mail regarding my diagnosis, I hadn't heard from her since. Then, on a Thursday night, Susie called me and said, "Guess what? I'm in Los Angeles on business, and although I can't stay all weekend, I want to come down to Orange County and see you."

I was shocked. Did she really want to drive down the 405 freeway on a Friday night? I replied, "Do you realize the traffic on a Friday night?"

She said, "I don't care. I'm here, and I want to see you, if it's a good time for you. If so, I'll see you sometime Friday night!"

She arrived around eight o'clock, and we spent the next few hours catching up, laughing, and reminding each other of why we were still friends over twenty-five years after we had first met in college. The thoughtfulness of these two friends touched me beyond words—Susie coming all that way just for a few hours and Ronna driving over two days just because she knew I needed her uplifting friendship at this uncertain time in my life. Not only did it give me a sense of true friendship and support, but these unselfish gestures did so much in the way of relieving Johnny too. He was free to go to work, take some time to go on some motorcycle rides with friends, and do his best to keep his own stress under control.

Chapter 6

MEETING WITH GOD, UH … I MEAN THE SURGEON

Since Ronna arrived on Sunday, she went with me for the second meeting with the surgeon. This gave Laura a chance to take a day off from the constant companionship she had been giving me. Additionally, it was great to have another pair of ears while discussing the upcoming surgery. Everyone was telling me that I needed to have a second opinion, so Ronna and I had some questions we wanted to ask the designated surgeon. Ronna was great to have with me, because like Laura she had some experiences that give her cause to stand up and ask the questions that need to be asked. I was so busy taking it in and dealing with my own emotions over what was being said that I couldn't ask the things I should have when I should have. But Ronna did.

We sat in the waiting room and talked about our years of friendship and how we would have never predicted that we'd be sitting together for an occasion such as this. Thankfully, Ronna always had a funny take on things and kept me laughing as we waited.

Finally we were called in to see the all-powerful one: the surgeon. At first there were the normal how do you dos, and then it seemed like we were finished. I was thinking, *Wait, I haven't really heard anything about the outcome.* Although he had said I would be fine, I hadn't heard much in the way of explanations.

Thank God Ronna was way ahead of me. She thought to ask him, "What about Tammy's lymph nodes?"

He replied without hesitation, "I will remove them."

Across the room Ronna and I shot a look at each other as if to say, "*What?*"

Then she asked him about the sentinel lymph node biopsy (SLNB), and he said, "I don't need that. In my experience if I'm doing a double mastectomy I take out the lymph nodes too, just to be on the safe side."

Again, Ronna and I were having trouble with this answer, and a look passed between us. She and I both knew that the SLNB should be required. We had done our homework and understood this test, where a radioactive substance, a blue dye, or both is injected into the breast via the nipples about an hour before the surgery. Then during the surgery a surgeon uses a device that detects radioactivity to find the sentinel node or looks for lymph nodes that are stained with the blue dye. Once the sentinel lymph node is located, the surgeon makes a small incision and removes the node. The sentinel node is then checked for the presence of cancer cells by a pathologist while the mastectomy is taking place. If cancer is found, the surgeon may remove additional lymph nodes. SLNB is usually done at the same time the primary tumor is removed. In addition to helping doctors stage cancers and estimate the risk that tumor cells have developed the ability to spread to other parts of the body, SLNB is helpful in avoiding more extensive lymph node surgery. Removing additional nearby lymph nodes may not be necessary if the sentinel node is negative for cancer. All lymph node surgery can have adverse effects, and some of these effects may be reduced or avoided completely if fewer lymph nodes are removed. Because breast cancer cells are most likely to spread first to lymph nodes located in the axilla, or armpit area, next to the affected breast, Ronna and I both recognized that because my tumors were located under my arms, this test would be vital to me.

As the surgeon turned to his computer and started adding notes, Ronna started peeking over his shoulder. From where she sat she could do that; I couldn't as I was on the exam table in front of him. As he typed, I asked him about a second opinion. I could tell by his tone of voice that this question did not sit well with him. "You already have a second opinion—your oncologist agrees with me."

This was not the second opinion I had in mind. Ever the research rat, Laura had already been doing some investigating for me and was concerned about how aggressive this surgeon was. Sunday night she had called to talk to Ronna and me about finding out about getting a second opinion outside of our health care provider. This guy's resistance to doing the sentinel node test along with his quick decision to remove all of my lymph nodes was just too much. He turned around and said we must perform the surgery quickly, before the cancer spread. He had scheduled me for the next week. That being said, I knew I had to get a second opinion and get it soon.

As we sat at lunch I asked Ronna about his response, and she heartily agreed with me. We both thought that he had his mind made up and was going to make sure I would do what he determined to be the best. Just to confirm this bad feeling, Ronna shared with me what she had seen on the computer screen; my oncologist had said that it could go either way. It was not a given that my lymph nodes needed to be removed. It really needed to be ascertained based on the SLNB. That certainly didn't sound like my oncologist was in total agreement with the surgeon.

The day ended with a call from the surgery scheduling department. My surgery was suddenly set for Thursday, July 26, only a few days away. Once again, I was struck with the thought that this surgeon was really pushing to get me in, perform a double mastectomy, and remove all of my lymph nodes much too quickly.

July 24, 2007

After I called Laura and gave her an update, she declared that I *had* to have a second opinion before going under the knife with this guy. She got on the phone and made an appointment for me to see a Dr. Harness at St. Joseph's Hospital. Not only was he one of their leading breast surgeons, but he was the head of the board of directors for their breast cancer center. It costs me close to a thousand dollars to see him, but it was worth it to have an expert outside of my own medical group. It was never a question about taking the money out of our account to cover the expense; it was necessary.

I called the surgery department back and told them I couldn't have surgery on Thursday because I was having a second opinion on that day. They were not very happy. The woman I spoke to said, "You know you need to get this done; you can't keep putting it off." That was such an uncalled-for comment. I wasn't putting anything off, just being thorough. After all, this was my body, my future, my life we were talking about. How rude!

The rest of the day was spent trying to get all the x-rays, notes, blood work, and other info that Dr. Harness would need to be able to determine the best course of action (in his opinion) for me . This was all very overwhelming to me. If it weren't for Ronna and Laura, I don't think I could have kept it all straight.

Sadly, the day came when Ronna had to leave to go back to Portland. She had been such a blessing and motivating companion; I was really going to miss her.

Ironically, that same day the surgeon's scheduling department called back and said that they had an opening for the following Friday and they were sending all the paperwork to my home for me to read and prepare for this surgery. I didn't mention the second opinion again. I had already learned that they didn't like to hear about that. I guess even though they "say" you can get one, it really challenges their authority.

I just thanked her and told her, "Actually, I may need to postpone my surgery and will contact you later." After a few more phone calls, I contacted that same office again to request the notes from my surgeon, and I was told by his nurse she had to get his permission to release them. My appointment was the next day, and I had been told that I needed those notes. Even after I drove over and asked in person that afternoon, I was told that he wouldn't release them. I was stuck, so I just decided to not worry about what had been said during the office visits. I knew I would not be using him anyway. I never did get those notes from that surgeon.

I can't even describe the feeling I had that afternoon—basically torn, unsettled, and afraid I might make the wrong decision. I had always been a decisive person; but this was so out of my comfort zone. This was the time I really had to trust that the Lord would lead me, show me, and comfort me. The last thing Ronna said to me as she was driving away was "Now is the time to get down on your knees and give it all to God." Humbly, I did.

Graciously, He answered …

> "When you pass through the waters, I will be with
> you; and when you pass through the rivers, they
> will not sweep over you" (Isaiah 43:2 NIV).

29

Chapter 7

A SECOND OPINION

July 26, 2007

After gathering as much information as I could for Dr. Harness I was ready for my second opinion. Laura and I were amazed at the night-and-day difference in the way I was treated by him and his staff compared to the previous week with my previous surgeon. There was no doubt in my mind that I had done the right thing. Even though I had balked at the price tag earlier, it wasn't even an issue now. Dr. Harness encouraged me to bring a tape recorder with me to make sure I understood everything that he was going to talk about. This was reassuring, because I had asked to do that with the other surgeon and he adamantly refused to allow a recording device in the room. So much is discussed that there is good chance much of it will be forgotten in a short time. Additionally, there is no way a person can remember everything that is discussed in order to share with family members not present for the meeting.

The first thing out of his mouth was how concerned he was that a woman my age, in good health, and with no bad health history could have a blood clot. He would have done a blood test to detect blood disorders as soon as he learned of the blood clot. "And furthermore," he said, "I wouldn't touch you in the ER until I knew what was going on there." His second area of concern was the whole lymph node removal. He was concerned that they weren't going to do any tests to determine if I needed any removed, much less all of them. Strike one.

Additionally, Dr. Harness was appalled that my current surgeon wanted to remove my lymph nodes without doing the sentinel node test first. He said, "Is he crazy? You could have all kinds of problems by removing the lymph nodes; lymphedema is a huge problem that could affect you for the rest of your life." Strike two.

Additionally, he was concerned that an MRI had not been ordered. He said that was a much better picture of what is going on in the body than just the pathology report. When I told him that when I had asked my current surgeon to order an MRI, he was shocked to learn that I was told, "No, we already know you have cancer in both breasts; it's not needed." Strike three.

There were many other things discussed. Time was on my side, and he felt that it was better to take more time and determine what was really going on rather than diving right in. He told me, "Your tumors have been growing for some time, and a matter of a few weeks is not going to make a big difference in your life." I absolutely did not need to have a double mastectomy in two days like the other surgeon had declared.

I was so elated to hear him say that that I almost missed the next warning he gave me. Knowing the cancer I had was estrogen receptive, any future cancers would feed off of any estrogen I produce. Unfortunately, the seeds had been sown. Once a window had been opened, it was possible that other cancer could follow. He asked me to seriously consider having a hysterectomy to eliminate any concerns of ovarian cancer. We would all like to think that by the time one goes through surgery, chemo, and everything else that usually follows, the body is cancer free. Now I was learning that there is always a chance of "C" coming back. Good grief!

As we prepared to leave, Dr. Harness pulled out his cell phone and looked up the phone number of a former student of his who was currently working for my healthcare provider. Not just any phone number—the surgeon's personal number! He told me to call him, tell him he sent me, and get an appointment with him. This surgeon did hundreds of sentinel node tests and most definitely knew what he was doing.

By the end of the meeting, my head was swimming with information, and I knew why they had suggested a tape recorder! I was armed with information and a sense of new power, and I knew what I needed to do. First thing in the morning, I would cancel my surgery and call the new surgeon and ask to be put on his surgery schedule.

Thank God for Laura being there with me, taking notes and tape recording the whole conversation. Needless to say I was having emotional thoughts during much of the discussion. Laura was able to ask questions that she knew should be asked, and she was able to remind me of things that I missed during our three hours with this caring and well-informed man. She giggled as we walked out and said, "I thought I was going to laugh out loud when he said, 'I eat, sleep, and breathe breasts.'"

Chapter 8

MAY THE FORCE BE WITH YOU

In many ways the weekends were a blessing to me. Since I hadn't had surgery yet and I wasn't able to make weekend calls to doctors and medical offices, I was able to enjoy "normal" things with my family. We attended Mariners Church, and each summer the church does a fun-themed series of messages related to summer blockbusters. One Sunday it was *Star Wars*. Although they used the theme, the message was full of scripture and Christian applications. It was well done, and I have to say this was probably the first time my son really listened! Ironically, one of the bonds I share with Craig is the love of *Star Wars* movies. I always took him to the theater to see the most recent *Star Wars* installment. Johnny was never a big fan, so it was an unexpected surprise to hear the title of that message. Additionally, Craig had not been asking too many questions about my illness, but knowing that he was a quiet kid I recognized that he was observing everything. Many times I would catch him listening in as I talked on the phone or told Johnny about the latest news. I was trying to stay very calm and give him a sense that I had it under control, even if I didn't! My son and I had always shared a special bond. He saw me as his rock, and I was determined to not let him down. It was a timely message for our whole family.

As I listened I was reminded that the Phantom Menace a la *Star Wars* is alive and well and doing all he can to make us fear. He whispers negatives, raises doubts, and generally adds fear to our lives. Of course he knows when to attack, and when we are down is the best time. That is exactly what I had been experiencing! As I sat and listened I realized that I didn't have to worry. The Force was with me! If God be for me, who then could be against me? I had always had a strong faith and awareness of my own salvation. Why was I suddenly forgetting that? There really was no way I could lose. If I made it through the battle, I won; if I didn't, I also won because I knew where I was going.

August 9, 2007

My new surgeon was a force to be reckoned with. He wasted no time in ordering an MRI for me. Since the MRI machine was located at UCLA, I decided I should enlist the help of my son. I told him that he could really help me out, because by taking him with me I would be able to use the carpool lane. I also saw this as a perfect opportunity to have a much-needed conversation with him. The ninety-minute car ride from Orange County to West Los Angeles was a great opportunity for my twelve-year-old son to hear from me what exactly was going on, something I felt he wanted to know but wasn't sure how to ask. He wanted to know if it hurt, and my immediate thought was, *Yes, the needles!* But instead I simply explained that there was some pain involved. He then asked, "Are you going to die?" Every child has that fear of losing a parent at one point or another, but my cancer was making the possibility more real. I told him that I had no intention of leaving him, but it would be up to what God had planned for me. Then, after some hesitation, he seemed to have an even bigger question. I prodded him, and he finally asked, "Will you lose your hair?" I had to smile at that one—isn't that the first question everyone wants to ask?

Craig waited in the empty waiting room, equipped with his ever-present Game Boy. Meanwhile I was entering the revered MRI inner sanctum. The MRI itself wasn't painful, not nearly as painful as the insertion of the ginormous IV port they stuck in my hand first to allow the contrast to be injected during the MRI. First they put me face down and got my breasts aligned into metal cups. This was extremely uncomfortable due to a protruding bone I have in the middle of my chest. I just couldn't find a spot where it didn't hurt. Since I had to lie still for several minutes, I was really hoping to find the "sweet" spot. With a bit more squirming around and fidgeting, I finally did. The magnetic resonance imaging machine was extremely loud, so loud that the technicians provided earplugs. I heard a series of clangs and clunks while the magnets whirled around, doing their job. Within an hour I had been resonated and Craig and I were back in the car-pool lane headed for home.

Tuesday I went to see the genetics counselor to have my blood drawn for the test. After they drew the vials I had to take them back to the counselor's office so she could send them off to the only lab in the country that does this test. Once the lab in Utah sent it back I would be called back and given the results and counseling based on what those results were. The counselor was very thorough, and she asked me lots of questions about my relatives, most of whose medical history I knew nothing about. Remarkably, no one on either side of my parents' families was used to sharing medical information. It was all very private, and even after they heard of my diagnoses I found myself dragging information out of them. I was shocked to find out that two of my father's sisters had already endured breast cancer. I was forty-five years old, and this was the first time I had heard this news. When I mentioned to my aunts that they might consider discussing genetic testing for my cousins, I was met with indifference. It made me realize how different we all are and how some people want to know and others do not.

Chapter 9

HAPPY BIRTHDAY TO ME

I felt so loved and special, thanks to my friends and family. Anyone going through this kind of ordeal needs the support of loved ones, which I certainly had. It's amazing how well my friends knew me and knew how to put a huge smile on my face. A few of my lovely gifts would serve as inspiration to get better fast so that I could enjoy using them. Johnny had been promising a special bike that would pay homage to my ordeal with breast cancer. He said, "The new scooter isn't finished yet, but just to keep you focused on getting better I have this for you." He then plopped a huge box on my lap. After tearing back the Christmas wrapping paper (that must have been the easiest paper to find without any help from me), I was thrilled to see a new full-faced *pink* helmet. I was delighted and told him as much. "I love it—I will feel like a 'Power Ranger' wearing it! Thank you."

Later that afternoon, I got a call from the surgery coordinator. She said that they had me on my new surgeon's surgery schedule for September 11, and if anything opened up before then, I would be notified. She said there were so many cancer patients waiting to be scheduled that I was lucky to even get that date. Unfortunately, because I was on a wait list I wasn't allowed to discontinue the injections (blood thinners) and begin the oral form. If I were to begin taking an oral form of blood thinner I would have to be off of it for a week before surgery and therefore would have to pass on any sudden surgery date that might become available. So it seemed that I was destined to remain a human pincushion.

The results from the MRI also came back. Just trying to be clever and light about the whole subject, I asked the person who called me, "Did I get a miracle and they were blank?"

Unfortunately the response was a dry "No, we see very clearly both of the cancers. They are still there. No miracle." … *Yet,* I thought.

I continued to read everything I could get my hands and eyes on and tried to do as much research as possible. Aside from the daily visits to the vampires (the blood draws), to make sure the blood thinners were still at an accurate level and the two daily injections of blood thinners themselves, I felt pretty good. In addition to the daily visits for blood draws I had an additional appointment scheduled for pre-op and a visit with the oncologist. I was thinking the dentist might be in order too, as I had read that the chemo does a number on the teeth.

Speaking of chemo, I think I was more afraid of that than the surgery itself. Most of what I had read led me to believe that most people experience a great deal of negative side effects in addition to the positive results of hopefully eradicating the cancer. I'm all for putting up a good fight, but what happens when you are beat up so badly during the battle that you can barely fight? The hair loss was not a big deal, and the fatigue should be okay to deal with since I had been told to take it easy by my new boss. Probably my greatest fear was how I would continue to be a mother and wife during the treatments. I had read enough to know that chemotherapy takes you to death's door and drops you off, and if possible you bring yourself back. A couple of people told me that they knew of situations where the patient did fine, but all of the information I was reading did not support that theory. The biggest factor seems to be what kind of cancer you have and at what stage. Ironically, I was so pleased with myself before all this happened for not having the flu or even a cold for over six years. That'll teach me to gloat.

August 18, 2007

On Saturday night I would have been having my annual "Leo" party in celebration of not only my own my birthday but the birthdays of my fellow August birthday friends. Instead Linda came to my house on Tuesday and we had lunch together and exchanged gifts. Having known each other since I was four years old and she was nine made this visit all the more enjoyable. She along with a couple of other dear girlfriends knew me so well that I didn't have to hide anything or act in front of them. She more than anyone was having a difficult time processing the news of my cancer diagnosis. She told me later that it was just so disturbing for her to even think of me as sick since we had shared our entire lives with each together. On that particular day, I would have never known that she was thinking that; she cheered me up with her sense of humor and shared funny quips that made me giggle. Just what the doctor ordered.

Although I had received some fabulous cards and wonderful gifts from my dear friends, the best gift was the news that I was scheduled for surgery the following Friday. My parents were still worried about all this, and they even called to offer to give me the money for me to go to Dr. Harness, the specialist at St. Joseph's. I told them that I felt comfortable with Dr. Harness's protégé and would never want them to pay for something as expensive as that. My sweet dad said, "We just want you to get the best treatment possible, and if it's something you need and can't afford, we will take it from our savings for you so you can get better."

I carefully said, "I appreciate your offering, but it's really not necessary, especially when I am blessed to have insurance! Dad, don't worry. I feel like I am in good hands now." This had to be extremely tough for them. Not only were they seventy years old, but to see their only child go through cancer was something that seemed to weigh so heavily on both of them. Certainly, if my own son was faced with this, it would break my heart. I am so glad and thankful it was me going through this and not my son, parents, or husband. So, happy forty-sixth birthday to me, and hopefully many more.

Chapter 10

I GOT THIS

The day before surgery, I went to the hospital for my pre-op appointment. It was a matter of having more blood work done and having more forms to fill out. Johnny had been administering my shots day and night, but thankfully, it was the last time I would need my injection of Lovenox. The concern was that my blood could not be too thin when I went into surgery; otherwise I could bleed to death. Without thinners, though, my clot would be free to travel, which made the situation complicated.

As I was filling out the forms I ran across a statement granting permission for "clowns to be in my room." Staring at the statement, I exclaimed, "*What!?*" The admission attendant explained that clowns came in to cheer patients up, but I needed to okay it before they would enter my room. Needless to say I didn't agree to this "visit." I told her, "*No,* absolutely not! If I wake up and find a clown in my room, I'll think I've died and gone to hell."

August 23, 2007

In preparation for the big day, I wrote cards to my sweet neighbors and friends and told them how much they mean to me. I also wrote cards to my parents, husband, and son. There were a few calls of encouragement, but if the truth be told, I found myself encouraging the caller more than the other way around. All I could do at that point was to pray for the calm that is needed to undergo surgery. I prayed for the surgeon, and I prayed for the peace that my family would need while waiting for the surgery to be completed. The rest was up to God. Ultimately, I was surrounded by love and support and lifted up in love by all the prayers from so many other friends and extended family. God prepared me for whatever was to be, and I felt completely at peace with that. Thank God for the peace that passes understanding.

I can honestly say that I was not nervous. I knew where I was going if I were to die. My only fear was that I would be leaving my son to grow up without a mom. Additionally, I knew how terrible it would be for my parents to lose their only child. Goodness, I was thinking in morbid terms—it was time to get to bed!

Chapter 11

FIRST WEEK AFTER SURGERY

By Tuesday I was finally up to writing an e-mail to my friends. Many of them had already sent cards and called. It was very difficult for me to hold the phone up to my ear for very long. I didn't have a speaker phone, and so I decided that the sooner I got an e-mail sent out the better. Many of them were forwarding the e-mails on to other relatives, and many had requested that I update them more often. Looking back, I realize that I was blogging and didn't even know what a blog was!

It was pretty amazing that only four days after surgery my biggest complaint was sore armpits. Of course I couldn't lift my arms, but there were very few things I needed to do that would require raising my arms. I was grateful for this considering how sore they would have been if I'd had all of my lymph nodes removed. Enduring the SLNB was excruciating. I kept reminding myself that I had really pushed for that test. When the needles full of dye were injected into my breasts about an hour before the surgery I was rethinking all that. Nothing can prepare you for having huge long needles shoved into each nipple ten times! No sedative was administered, because it would slow down the rate that the dye could travel and therefore the lymph nodes would not be viewable by the time the surgeon needed to test the lymph nodes. It was something I will never forget but wish I could. Ultimately it was worth the pain, because no cancer was found in any of my lymph nodes and therefore I was spared their removal and the aftereffects of that removal later in my life.

Although I didn't had the nerve to look at my chest area after the surgery, I did take a makeshift shower Monday night. Johnny and I took off the lavender tube top that was in place when I awoke from surgery and covered the bandages with a light towel. Although I hadn't seen the actual site, I could tell that it was rather concave in that area, something no one ever mentioned and a discovery that I certainly wasn't expecting. I knew that I had to brace myself for the experience of seeing it for the first time. Going from a 36 DDD to a 34 "nothing" would be something to get used to. I remember developing at an early age and looking in the mirror at my profile to see the changes in my body. Here I was, doing the same thing thirty-three years later.

Mom and Dad were at the house with Johnny, Craig, and me. It was too far for my parents to drive back and forth from Oceanside, an hour away. My wonderful neighbors were also pitching in to take care of our Yorkie, Tiki, and Craig. Since I had been in the hospital for three days it was a relief to finally be home. Although Johnny had arrived at the hospital fully intending to drive me home, he had driven his truck. There was no way I could climb up into a truck with my bandages, drains, and sore arms. Luckily, my dad immediately volunteered to drive me home in his car. My dad was so gentle when he placed the seatbelt on me. As he did so, I lifted my hand up to keep the belt from pressing on my now flattened and tender chest. As he slid into the driver's seat, he smiled with tears in his eyes and said, "You're gonna be all right. I love you, Tam."

Johnny and Craig led the way home in the truck, and my parents and I followed. My little Yorkie was at the front door to welcome me home. I was too afraid of her jumping on me and perhaps pulling out my drains or, worse yet, jumping on my stitches. So, instead of my usual greeting of "Come see Momma," I just told her I missed her and then made my way into my bedroom. Craig reached down and scooped Tiki up, and the two of them went off to the kitchen to see what kind of treats my mom had made for them. Meanwhile, Johnny began to prepare the injection for my next dose of blood thinner, since I still couldn't start the pill form for a while. My mom cooked dinner for us, and my dad was lifting my spirits even though I knew he was dealing with his own fears and concerns. After all, I was a daddy's girl, not to mention his only child.

Since I was encouraged to get up and move around I did make my way out of the comfort of my bedroom and venture into the living room.

One afternoon about a week after my surgery I was sitting on the end of the couch and Johnny came home from work eager to see how I was doing. In his exuberance he plopped down on the couch practically on top of me. My drain tubes stretched against my skin, and I felt a piercing pain next to where they were stitched into the skin. As I shrieked out in pain, my dad lunged toward me trying to help, and Johnny leaped back off of the couch apologizing profusely. In all this excitement, our dog Tiki thought it was time to play and tried to jump up on me and give me kisses. In all the confusion, my mom started to shout at Tiki, which made her want to jump onto my lap for comfort. As my dad removed all six pounds of Tiki from my lap, I got up and scurried back to the shelter of my bedroom. Later, sitting on the edge of the bed, I started to think that perhaps because I was up and about and trying to seem "normal" I gave the impression that all was well. However, my healing was still taking place, and certainly in regards to my emotional healing I was far from finished. Although I had given a big talk about "being more than my breasts" and being prepared *to die,* I wasn't really prepared *to live,* to live in this new body. That would take more time and perhaps much more time than any of the physical recovery would.

Pain management wasn't too difficult. I tried to only take two pain pills a day, one at night before bed and one when I woke up. During the day I felt a bit achy but had no extreme pain. Additionally, I was dragging around those "drains" that were hanging at the end of long tubes that were inserted during the surgery, an evil necessity due to the amount of fluids the body produces after such an invasive surgery as this. At the end of each tube there was a hand-grenade-sized bulb that collected the fluids. Each bulb needed to be emptied and its output logged daily. What a cumbersome nightmare to contend with. Swinging from under each arm like two extra appendages, they had to be carefully negotiated lest the fluid bulb become separated from its tube. At some point the fluid would become clear and they could be removed.

I shuddered to think how many more drains would have been required if they had removed all of my lymph nodes. In addition to having the drains removed in a week or so, I would also go see the oncologist in order to discuss chemo treatments. Graciously, he was giving me a few weeks to recover before beginning the treatments. In an effort to make this more tolerable, I decided to ask him about chocolate chemo; "essence of chocolate" would make it so much more appealing.

Chapter 12

FORTY-EIGHT-HOUR ROLLER-COASTER RIDE

September 6, 2007

Thursday morning Laura took me to get the tubes and drains removed. She dropped me at the front of the hospital and said that she would meet me upstairs. She parked the car as I made my way over to the elevator. The ride up was odd, as people were staring at me with pained looks on their faces. I thought they must be looking at my concave chest. The waiting room was full and running over with patients. There was nowhere for me to sit, so I stood in the hall in my short, summer robe, careful not to bump into anything as I walked down the hallway in search of a place to stand out of the way. As I walked, I noticed people still staring at me. I know I didn't have any makeup on and my hair was a mess since I could not comb it with my sore arms, but did I really look that bad? As soon as Laura arrived, I found out what the problem was. As she walked up, she started to giggle and said, "Oh, dear. We really should have pinned those tubes and drains up into your gown." Realizing what she was talking about, I looked down at my now very full drainage bulbs and their ugly feeding tubes. They were hanging down by my knees for all the world to see. No wonder I had gathered so many looks on my way to the waiting room. Fortunately, my name was called just then.

The nurse told us that this was a relatively simple procedure and that she would be doing it. No doctor needed today. She then began to unwrap my bandages. She oohed and aahed as she did so and asked me

44

if I had seen it yet. I told her no, and she said, "Oh, well, today will be the day then!" I was not sure I was ready for that, but it didn't matter, because in the next second I was wracked by a pain I hadn't ever felt before. As Laura held my hand, she saw the look on my face when the left tube came out. It was the kind of pain that sucks the wind out of you. I was unable to breath, much less speak for a few seconds afterward. She immediately leaned over and said a prayer over me before the right tube was removed. Amazingly, the right tube and drain removal was different. It was "uncomfortable" but certainly bearable compared to the left drain experience. It seems that the left tube was jammed next to a nerve and that nerve was irritated as the tube slid past it on its way out of my body. The fact that the nurse was trying to do it slowly made it even more painful; it was no fault of hers.

After the drains were removed, the nurse leaned over and produced a mirror that was on the table nearby. She held it up and asked me if I wanted to look. Again, Laura saw the pained look on my face. This time, Laura reached down and brought her camera out of her bag. She leaned forward with the camera and then took a picture of my chest. She looked at the picture, looked at me, and then turned the camera around for me to see the picture. This gesture of sensitivity and understanding allowed me to view my disfigured body with an element of emotional distance. After objectively studying the picture for a few moments, I was ready to take the mirror from the nurse and look at myself for the first time. Having prepared myself by seeing the picture first, I wasn't nearly as traumatized by my own reflection as one would expect.

The nurse commented on what a wonderful and valuable asset Laura was to me. She went on to tell us about how many women she saw coming in for treatment all alone. I recognized without a doubt that I would have been a mess without Laura. She was my rock, and once again she showed the grace of God through her actions. It would seem natural to depend on one's spouse to be the rock. In my case I didn't have that expectation, due to my husband's personality. As long as I had known Johnny, he was all about creating fun and memorable experiences and seemed to avoid uncomfortable situations. He was the life of the party and always made things "fun." My illness was completely out of his comfort zone, and we all knew that it most definitely was *not* fun. Laura, on the other hand, was my tender yet practical friend. Nothing seemed to faze her. She put her faith in her

Savior and stood on the foundation that gave her strength. She was not only a warrior for herself and all life had dished out to her but had become my number one advocate.

My roller coaster took another turn when I started the pill form of blood thinners. This required me to have my blood checked daily for about a week until they got the dose straight. This must be done before 10:00 each morning, even over the weekend. That being said, I was still having the injections twice a day in the stomach. After a week I would be required to go in only twice a week for blood checks and then perhaps once a week. Once again I felt like a human pincushion.

After receiving that news, I gave my new boss a call to fill her in. She said without hesitation, "You need to just stay home and take care of all these things. Don't worry about coming back in here. I'll take care of the paperwork for you to be off until you are finished with all your treatments."

As much as I appreciated her saying that, I was still nervous about not being there. After all, I had just started and was already calling in sick! Looking back on it, I realize that this was a gift that I did not fully understand or appreciate at the time. I wish I had completely let go of any guilt and just focused on healing.

Please stay seated at all times; the coaster will make sharp turns.

Sitting on the couch across from my parents, I got a call from my surgeon. He called to say he had received the pathology report. He said it was highly unusual (why am I beginning to flinch every time I hear that phrase?), but unfortunately, the pathology report found a third cancerous tumor. Although he thought he had removed everything, he did not know about this tumor so he didn't remove its "margins." He told me that I now needed radiation because of this "unfortunate" discovery. I can't tell you how my heart fell when I heard him say this. As we said good-bye and I was hanging up the phone I heard him say, "I am so sorry." This time I was unable be upbeat, and the tears streamed down my face.

My parents could see my face change as the doctor spoke to me. I knew that they wanted to know what was going on, and I had to find my voice to tell them the news. I cried harder at this news than any so far. My parents were stunned. They had been so supportive of me and told me not to worry, but they could tell how disappointed I was. Up until then I had felt that the end of the tunnel was near; now it seemed to stretch on forever. This changed everything about any reconstruction I may have been able to do after chemo.

The roller coaster just took a plunge, and I struggled to hang on.

By the end of that eventful week I was actually feeling better and felt that it was time for my parents to return to their own home in Oceanside. They had certainly been helpful, taking care of the cooking and cleaning needs of Craig and Johnny. They made sure I was happy and cared for as best they could. But it was time for these two precious seventy-year-olds to get back to their own doctors' appointments, plants, and church activities. I almost cried as we said our good-byes. When my dad gave me a hug, he was so gentle and careful not to embrace me too tightly. My mom kissed me and repeated several times that I should call them if I needed anything. She also wanted me to tell her again when Laura would be back over; she trusted Laura. As much as my parents loved Johnny as a son-in-law, after the couch incident they had a strong suspicion that it would be Laura who would be my guardian and helper in their absence.

Chapter 13

GEARING UP AND MELTING DOWN

Finally some good news: The oncologist said that the pathology report stated that my tumors (all three of them) were stage I, not stage II as originally thought in the biopsy. Because of that, my radiation treatment would be a shorter version of what is usually done but was still a necessary component of my treatment. I was told in no uncertain terms that if the cancer came back to the chest wall, it would be inoperable; therefore, every possible tactic must be employed. My oncologist then shifted gears and began to discuss the type of chemo he had planned for me. I learned that the chemo treatment always depends on what kind of cancer you have, what stage the cancer is in, and your age. With those factors in my mind the doctor told me that I would get, in his words, "the big guns." My treatment would definitely be the kind that makes hair fall out, generates mouth sores, and of course destroys white blood cells. I guess he was trying to prepare me. He said, as I was leaving, "Don't worry; you won't have to begin chemo until after you've had a chance to heal from the radiation." Goody, I could hardly wait.

Finally a bit of great news: I was done taking the Lovenox injections for the blood clot. Switching over to the tablets of Warfarin was so much easier on me, and although I still had to go have blood draws every day, I didn't have to have the extra two shots in my stomach, Hallelujah! Warfarin is basically rat poison and is extremely dangerous to ingest. That's why the blood tests were needed every day to make sure I took exactly the amount needed for medicinal purposes—like I would really be taking this for any other reason!

"A merry heart doeth good like a medicine"
(Proverbs 17:22 NKJV).

September 7, 2007

I had a meltdown. I was lying in bed fuming over the state of the house as well as the attitude of my husband. The longer I lay there, the madder I got. I decided that I needed to clear the air. In a nutshell I told Johnny how upset I was over everything and that if he didn't want to help me get through this, I would understand and I would let him out of the whole marriage. I told him that I refused to go through this and have to take care of him too. If he wasn't going to help me, he was basically hurting me, and I couldn't take another day of it.

Of course he was in shock and told me to calm down. I told him I was calm and had thought a lot about this. When he wanted to know exactly what he'd done to upset me, I was ready with a list. I spat, "All the dishes are piled up, you aren't making sure Craig does his homework, and you haven't even talked to me about how I feel. You just tell everyone I'm great and assume I am." I took a breath and continued on, "All day I have to take care of medical issues and phone calls from doctors, nurses, and people wanting to know how I am. You aren't handling any of it, and you aren't even asking me if I need help with it." We just stared at each other, and then I saw him glance at the TV! That pushed me over the edge. I moved in for one more attack: "I can't believe you practically sat on me just days after I had returned from the hospital!"

He stammered, "I just wanted to sit close to you."

My response was not kind or understanding. I sneered and replied, "You hurt me when you sat on the right side of me. I was still in bandages and in pain!"

Johnny dropped his head down, and then he looked me right in the eye and said, "I know you don't mean it. I know it's just the cancer talking."

Outraged, I turned on my heel and stomped back to the bedroom. I was livid, and he was unflappable. Ever the optimist, he would not accept responsibility for any of what I had just dumped on him. Although I grumbled to myself about how he just didn't get it and I was mad for the next couple of days, I have to admit that from then on he seemed to be more aware of the situation and what I needed from him. Unfortunately, it was on the heels of a very ugly exchange. Sadly, I hadn't held anything back. I later regretted this outburst, but at the time I felt I just had to get it out and give him what I felt at the time was a wakeup call.

September 8, 2007

Wouldn't you know it; I started my period. Perhaps that explains the outrageous meltdown. But then again, it's not like I had a normal week. When I saw my surgeon, he was very pleased with the way the skin was healing and thought the scar looked good too. Again, he said he was so sorry about the third tumor being found. He realized that I didn't want to have to do radiation but reminded me that I had to do it to be on the safe side. He had made arrangements for me to speak to a radiation-oncologist the following week. He also recommended that I do the radiation before doing the chemotherapy. I didn't understand that, and I feared that it might disrupt my leave at work. I only had so much time available to me. Unfortunately, radiation must be performed every day, and there were only two available facilities. Neither facility was close. One was located in Hollywood on Sunset Blvd, and the other was in Ontario. Neither facility would be convenient such that I would be able to go to work afterward.

Somewhat later than I should have received it, I got a new camisole to wear. It was made out of very soft cotton and came with "fluffs" to replace my nonexistent breasts. Replace is an optimistic term for sure. The fluffs looked weird and were difficult to get positioned. Having never "placed" breasts before, I wasn't sure where they should go. Most of the time, I just pulled the stuffing out and wore the camisole alone. Additionally, there were two pouches inside the camisole to hold the drains. Where was this camisole two weeks earlier when I had drains? This should have been something I received when I left the hospital! At the very least I should have had it when I had the tubes and drains in and was traipsing out for blood work and going to the hospital daily. There are so many things that no one prepares a woman for during this process. Unfortunately, much of my knowledge was gained as I went.

My surgeon finally gave me the thumbs-up on driving. I drove myself to get my daily blood draws and to my other appointments that week. Feeling like I had a bad sunburn, I wound up holding the seat belt away from my chest. Unfortunately, I experienced another difficult blood draw; once again the phlebotomist just couldn't hit a vein. She finally went to the arm that had the clot in it. This particular woman had twenty-five years of experience, so I just had to trust her. I told her, "Go for it. Anything is better than this painful poking!" Thankfully, she was successful.

On Wednesday I was accompanied by my friend Linda, to the follow-up consultation with the genetics specialists. The results had come back from the blood test, and the specialist said that the genes that were tested came back *negative*. She also said that there would be no immediate need for a hysterectomy (as previously discussed) but that I may have a genetic defect undetectable at this point in medical testing. She said, "It's interesting the way genetic testing works; we can only test the genes we know about. There may very well be other genetic mutations that occur, be we aren't aware of them yet. So when I tell you the tests came back negative, that's based on what we as scientists know now." I wasn't sure about how I felt given that knowledge. But since I did know that my tumors were estrogen-positive receptors, I would have to consider that information in the future.

Although I had been told by my oncologist that the radiation would be before chemo and I might have a lighter dose, I soon received contradictory information. I learned that you don't count on anything for too long. Thursday I had the appointment with the radiation-oncologist. He was a very unique man and had everything prepared that he wanted to say. When I tried to ask a question, he put his hand up and said, "In a minute. Let me finish what I have to say first." So I sat back and listened to him talk about why radiation was necessary. By the time he finished, I had forgotten what I wanted to ask, and of course I thought of it later. I wish Laura had been with me; she would have been writing it all down for our discussion later. Since she had her own life and family to attend to, I was trying to not ask her to do as much for me now that I could drive myself. If I had been thinking better, I would have taken my tape recorder with me to that appointment.

The radiologist recommended six weeks of radiation (the shortest possible treatment). Yikes! Watching my face drop, he told me, "I want you to have your chemotherapy first." I was happy to hear that, since I was hoping to complete chemo by Christmas. If all went well and my blood count stayed high enough to complete the treatments, that was a real possibility. An answered prayer for sure. Thank you, God.

Once I had seen the radiologist, I put a call in to the oncologist's office to get the ball rolling. Every day I started to feel better. I even went to church on Sunday. Finding something to wear was my biggest issue. I wouldn't get any prostheses till the end of the following week, and I gave up on those little pillows designed to tuck into my camisole. They were more trouble than they were worth; each time I got out of the car and unbuckled my seatbelt I would have to readjust my "breasts."

I continued to have visits from family, friends, and neighbors. One of my friends even decided that I needed a "makeover" and cut my hair. She said I couldn't reach the back to comb my shoulder-length hair properly, so why have it to worry about? After she cut my hair, she said, "I'm exhausted. I need a nap." At first I thought she was just kidding with me, but she wasn't! To my amazement, she proceeded to go crawl into my bed. As she pulled up the covers she said, "Make sure and wake me up in two hours." After that day I would laugh each time I saw my reflection in a mirror. It reminded me of her visit and her act of "exhausting" kindness.

"And My God will meet all your needs according to his glorious riches in Jesus Christ" (Philippians 4:19 NIV).

Chapter 14

TAKING "THE GIRLS" TO VEGAS

September 19, 2007

The day for the chemotherapy consultation arrived. The new facility was only a few months old, and I was blessed to be going there for my treatments instead of the old facility several miles away, which was already overbooked with over eight hundred patients. There were many things that could happen with chemo that I was completely unaware of. Because it lowers the body's resistance to germs, I learned that I would have to be extremely careful, and additional blood draws would be necessary before and after each treatment. My oncologist was observing many things during that time, especially my white blood cell count. If my white count dropped too far, they might consider giving me an additional medication designed to boost it. If the numbers didn't improve, the chemo treatments would have to be postponed.

Additionally there were things like numbness, loss of balance, jaw pain, hearing loss, vision changes, stomach pain, diarrhea, and constipation. Then of course, there's the more common and talked-about side effects: loss of appetite, nausea, loss of hair, and mouth sores. There were plenty of other things the counselor talked about that after a while just made my head swim. I missed having Laura with me at the appointment. It is amazing how much is missed when the mind starts getting emotionally involved. When Laura was in attendance, I always knew that she would have all of the information carefully documented and would present it to me again later, thus allowing me to digest it in smaller, bite-sized pieces. Since Laura wasn't with me at this appointment, I was thankful to be given a folder full of notes that I could take home and read on my own. I had a feeling I would need to review them several times.

My first treatment of Taxotere and Cytoxan began on a Friday. Before each treatment I would have to begin taking steroids. Then I received steroids during the treatment; for every bag of Taxotere and bag of Cytoxan (my "cocktail"), I received a bag of steroid "chaser." Due to the large amount of steroids and because of the cancer drugs' side effects I was told to expect weight gain. I had been trying for so long to lose the weight I had gained from being off my feet the previous year; a grueling time recuperating from three foot surgeries, and now I had to accept more weight. At this point I wasn't sure how much weight they were talking about. In my opinion, any weight gain was unacceptable, but I wasn't given a choice.

Not wanting to waste precious time, my friend Cathy decided that she needed to get me away. Realizing that I had just a few days before everything would change in my life, she suggested that we go to Las Vegas, Nevada. It's a four-hour drive from her house, and for several years we had been making the trip at least once a year. Considering that we had been friends since we were ten years old, it was an enjoyable tradition for us middle-aged gals to maintain. It seemed fitting to go at this time, even if it was just to see the difference between this time and our previous trips. Before we left, I was able to go into the breast shop and get my new prosthetic breasts. I explained to the manager of the store about my upcoming trip to Vegas. She was very kind and told me that she would fit me for my new breasts. If they had them in stock I could walk out of there wearing them. In addition to a shop full of every shape, size, and color of pseudo breasts imaginable, there was an assortment of specialty clothing items. There were hundreds of different styles of bras, most of which were cut pretty far up on the chest in order to hide the scars and concaveness. There were stylish tops and bathing suits and numerous soft camisoles equipped with the practical drain pockets. Seeing all the paraphernalia, once again I realized how much more was required in the treatment and adjustment to the evil breast cancer. It seemed that breast cancer was the gift that kept on giving. By the time I left the shop I had two pairs of new "girls"—an everyday

day pair to wear with clothes and a pair that would fit into the new mastectomy swimsuit that I also purchased. *Vegas, here I come!*

Johnny said he would take care of things at home. Craig had started middle school, and Tiki needed walking, food, and water.

With my new bathing suit, fake boobs, and a desire to get away from it all, I drove to Cathy's house. From there we left for Vegas. Cathy had arranged two nights in a deluxe suite at a brand-new hotel in Las Vegas. Our first night in town, Cathy said, "Hey, we have got to drive down the strip. It's going to be a while before you get back here, and by the time we do get back again you know there will be three new hotels erected and at least two ancient ones will be imploded!"

We crept down the strip and pulled in to the very opulent driveway of the Bellagio. As the valet opened the door for us I caught Cathy's eye as she winked and said, "I hope you are hungry and ready for the dancing waters!" We promenaded through the extravagant casino and made our way to one of the most impressive places to eat in Las Vegas: Olive's restaurant. Located inside the Bellagio, it is known for having the desirable front-row seats to the iconic dancing waters show. The very coveted tables out on the balcony overlook the Bellagio Lake, where every fifteen minutes guests are treated to a grand display of lights and sky-high waters dancing in time to exquisite music. It's spectacular, and we were right there at the front of the balcony, seated at the center table to enjoy it all. Beyond the dancing waters a perfect view of the magical lights of the Las Vegas strip twinkled. It was more than enough to make me forget all about the upcoming medical procedures. We spent the time giggling, joking, and enjoying the hot Las Vegas night—the calm before the storm.

Chapter 15

CHEMICAL WARFARE

My treatment would be every three weeks. If the blood draws showed that my white cells were down too far, the next treatment would be postponed for a week. Chemotherapy works because it is very systematic. If the treatment needed to be postponed more than once, unfortunately then a whole new chemo treatment plan would have to be calculated. Additional blood draws would be every week and sometimes twice a week depending on how it went.

I had a whole panel of blood drawn so that there would be a baseline for the next day's treatment. I was still on those hateful blood thinners, and of course that factored into the whole treatment plan as well.

The planner in me was inspired; I carefully assembled a tote bag full of supplies to take with me to my first chemo: my journal, iPod, tissues, water bottle, light snacks, light blanket, phone, and one of the books my friend Linda just brought me. I was ready. Those were things they recommended to bring, I found out later that there were a few additional things I might need as well, like a personal fan for when the chemicals and I didn't get along. Also, the chemicals tend to make the patient's mouth flare up, so drinking a really cold drink seemed to help. During one of my treatments, a very thoughtful woman came in with Slurpees for everyone! My favorite! I was instantly transported back to that first wonderful job at 7-Eleven. Smiling as I accepted one, I then proceeded to "slurp" my way through chemo.

Although my oncologist told me that my hair wouldn't begin to fall out until after two chemo treatments, he suggested that I go look at wigs while I still felt well enough to do it. There was a wig store right next to the prosthetic breast store. Thanks to my friend Deb and the recent haircut she had given me, I decided I might as well look at several different styles. There was no need for me to stick to the shoulder-length bob I had worn for the last few years. I was also thinking I might as well take a look at red, platinum, and brunette wigs too! I had been a blonde all my life, and if there was ever going to be time to experiment it would be now.

September 21, 2007

In preparation for my first chemo treatment, I had to go in for additional blood work and begin the steroids the day before. Although I was told to take them three times a day, taking the last two tablets at night right before bedtime apparently was misinformation. Consequently, I was awake all night long, not nervous, as one would expect, but completely wired and unable to sleep.

When I arrived for my treatment, I told the nurse about being awake all night. She said, "What time did you take your last pre-chemo pills?"

I told her before bed, and she said, "No! That's not what you should have done. They are a stimulant, and you need to take them absolutely *no later* than 6:00 p.m." Again, learning as I go.

My blessing for the day was having my lifelong friend Renee with me to take the edge off my nerves and spend the day with me. We had a joke between us that I got paid to talk and she got paid to listen. She is an international court reporter, and I didn't get to see her very often due to her hectic schedule. She was always traveling for her job and quite often was out of the country. Time was very precious to her, so I truly appreciated her taking off the entire day just for me. She drove the two hours down the 405 freeway from the San Fernando Valley and didn't go home until after she had cooked a wonderful Italian dinner for us that night.

Renee and I have known each other all our lives. She delights in telling other people that we have been friends since World War II. When they give her a puzzled look, she smiles and says, "On April 29, 1945, the US Army liberated Dachau, the first concentration camp established by the Nazis. My uncle and Tammy's grandfather were in the Forty-Second Rainbow Division, the division that liberated a subcamp of

Dachau that same day. After the war ended, my uncle and Tammy's grandfather remained good friends, and when both families moved to California from the East Coast, they not only continued their own friendship but united their families in friendship too. Our mothers then became close friends, and once they married, the husbands were invited into the friendship too. Eventually Tammy and I were born, exactly one month apart." By this time most people were usually staring at her with a total look of shock and amazement. Meanwhile she would be beaming, knowing that once again she had amused her listener as well as exposed the splendid family history that she and I shared. That day was no different, and as Renee spent all day with me, I was delighted to hear her share our story at least twice that day.

Renee was such a great distraction for that first chemotherapy. The needle they used was enormous, and it was inserted in my left arm near the bend in my elbow. It hurt quite a bit going in, and then I started to turn bright red. Within seconds I began to have an allergic reaction to the drugs. My nurse ran down the hall to get my oncologist. She came running back saying, "Your doctor said we have to give you some Benadryl first and then regulate the drip so that it transfers the chemicals very slowly." It took six and a half hours. Most people's day in the chemo chair lasts about four hours. Thank God I had Renee with me to make the day fly by.

Monday I was supposed to go back to work. I had been gone since July, and it was the end of September. The chemo was supposed to really take effect on the third day, the day I was scheduled to begin work. Since this was my first treatment, I had no idea what to expect. However, I felt that I needed to go back because I still had radiation to contend with and I couldn't afford to run out of hours. Having hours meant staying on the books, staying on the books meant getting a paycheck, getting a paycheck meant my health insurance was being paid, and paying for my health insurance meant I could complete the treatments I had planned. And we all knew how important completing the treatments was.

Surprisingly, Sunday I felt well enough to attend the Susan G. Komen "Walk for the Cure" in Orange County. Several people had mentioned it to me and suggested that if I felt well enough I should try to attend. Indeed, it was a moving experience to be among so many other survivors. One question kept going through my head as Johnny and I took it all in: "When do I get to say I am a survivor?" There were so many women wearing banners and signs stating how many years they had been cancer free. There were a few runners who had signs on their backs saying who they were running for, many of whom had not survived. That was a sobering sight, one I didn't want to ask or think about at that point in time. Overall, it was very inspiring to be there, and I felt that I was among friends. Having Johnny and my little dog Tiki there with me made me feel like I was being supported even if I wasn't calling myself a survivor yet. Never wanting to miss an opportunity to dress for the occasion, Tiki wore her pink outfit and matching hair ribbons in support of me.

By the third day, chemo was rearing its ugly head, but I wasn't going to let it win. Although my boss kindly told me I could take the day off from work, I still had a few errands to run. Although these errands didn't require me to travel far, I found myself getting lost. I would make wrong turns and then not know where I was going. By the end of the day, I felt extremely tired and worn out. Initially, my oncologist tried to convince me to stay home for the duration of the chemo treatments but finally gave me the green light to go back to work, which is where I was expected to be the next day. Nevertheless, I just wasn't sure I had the energy for it. How blessed I was to have a supervisor who said that she would support me no matter what I decided to do.

September 25, 2007

People at work were so happy to see me and gave me so many positive words of encouragement. Once again I was surrounded by wonderful people who only wanted to show their concern and support. Although I actually made it through the day, I was drained and started getting a sore throat, both side effects that I had been warned about.

My day started at 8:00 in the morning, and I wound up leaving around 4:00 that afternoon. During the day I spent many hours reading and responding to e-mail as well as spending time with my (still new to me) boss. Ever gracious, she said to me, "I want you to play this by ear; don't overdo it. If you feel like you need to go home, just let me know and get on out of here."

I told her how much I appreciated her saying that, and when I told her I would be fine, she said, "Well, you don't really know yet, so remember that your health comes first, and don't worry. I can get by without you for a while. We didn't have you or anyone else in this position before, so don't worry—we will just postpone the things you were going to do until a little bit later." Her telling me that was so freeing to me. I had been carrying around so much guilt about not being able to be there, and she took away those negative feelings with her kind words. I realized again how blessed I was to have such a strong supportive boss, unlike some bosses.

Even though I was extremely fatigued by the time I got home, my work was not finished. I still had to cook dinner and oversee homework. Also, I received a notice that parent-teacher conferences were being scheduled. That's one of those things that I would have to do. It didn't matter what else was going on; certain things still needed to happen. My son had already been struggling with going into middle school, and it seemed like he was just barely making a passing grade in his new classes. As much as I tried not to worry about things, his education was something that haunted my thoughts. What if he failed a whole semester or year because I wasn't spending the time I should have spent with him during these trying years? The homework was tough and plentiful. It seemed that he would not, or perhaps could not, do it without some prodding. Johnny was never one to help with homework; his numerous attempts to help usually ended in fighting and Craig's tears. I determined by the time Craig was in fifth grade that I must be the one to take charge of overseeing homework assignments. So before I could crawl into my bed, I was determined to look at Craig's assignments and complete the parent-teacher conference request. Eventually I was able to make my way to my bed. My day was done, thank God.

Chapter 16

HAIR TODAY, GONE TOMORROW

The next week I started noticing more hair in my hands after I shampooed. By Wednesday I noticed that I was picking a lot of hair off my blue chair at work. One Friday when I met two friends for lunch I was mortified when they walked up to greet me outside the restaurant and Bill reached over to pull a long blonde hair off my shoulder. He just looked at me and smiled a knowing smile. Brandi was too busy regaling us with one of her funny stories to notice what had just happened, but I couldn't stop thinking about it. It was so absorbing to me that all through lunch I just kept thinking, *It's already happening! He told me two treatments. Why is it already happening!*

As of Saturday the hair was in my mouth, hanging off my purse strap that had been on my shoulder, and covering my clothes as if I owned a Samoyed dog. It started to occur to me that it would not be wise for me to be around a buffet or even prepare meals for others. It was gross enough to have my own hair in my mouth and on my plate, so I shuddered to think how someone else would feel to find my hair in their food. My friend Norma came to the rescue. She walked across the street to visit me on Saturday and listened to me tell her about my current situation. She smiled her captivating smile and said, "No problem, mi amiga, I will cut your hair just like I cut my whole family's hair. When you're ready, come over, I will take care of it for you." And then she trotted back across the street to her house.

I took one last look in the mirror and told Johnny what was going to happen and walked out the door. He said, "Wait for me. I'll take pictures!"

When I knocked on her door, she was already waiting for me with a cape, her scissors, and her electric razor. She reached out to hug me and said, "No worries, my friend."

I thought to myself, *Easy for her to say. Her hair grows so fast she can have a pixie hair cut at the beginning of summer and have hair all the way down her back by Christmas.* My hair was not so quick to grow. I had been growing it for several years and still only had it just past my shoulders. All the waviness of my hair kept it very stylish but at the same time caused it to grow very slowly. Realizing that this was going to happen whether I wanted it to or not, I said, "Okay, let's do this," and sat down in the chair in front of her.

By this time, Craig and Norma's son and daughter popped their heads into the room and said they wanted to watch. Johnny stood in the corner of the room with the camera, and Norma began to cut. As soon as she started to cut with the scissors, I started to cry. Stopping to hug me and reassure me, she put the scissors down and reached for the electric razor. As my tears continued to fall, she began to shave off the remaining blonds locks. Her ever-present smile and murmurings of "It's okay, mi amiga, it's okay..." gave me comfort and the realization that this was a moment in time I would never forget. I began to laugh a little, and as I looked into her face I saw that she was crying too. Together we laughed through the tears as my hair hit the floor. Meanwhile Johnny was snapping away as the kids stood in the doorway in amazement.

When Norma finally put the razor down, she handed me a mirror and said, "Well, what do you think?" My immediate response was not good. I was disappointed to see how misshapen my head was. This was the first time I had really seen the actual shape of my skull, and it wasn't anything like the beautiful bald women I had seen pictures of in *National Geographic*. No, my head was completely flat in the back. One thing was clear to me: I needed to get out and get a wig soon, the next day if possible! I had a couple of scarves and one helmet cap designed for women to keep their hair in place while wearing a motorcycle helmet. That would have to do for the time being. The other observation I had was how much colder my head was without my hair covering my scalp. That would soon end due to the heat produced by the steroids and chemo. Before long I would throw all vanity to the wind in favor of an air-conditioned scalp.

As of Friday when I had my last blood draw, I still had a very low white cell count. So it was back to the Cipro and a restricted diet (nothing but overcooked food). I never thought I'd be missing salads and fruit so much. I hadn't thrown up at all after the first chemo, and I was told that this particular chemo "cocktail" was not known for that. On the contrary, this chemo treatment was known for making the patient gain weight; just my luck I get the "cupcake chemo."

My oncologist decided to give me a shot to boost my white cells. It involved my bone marrow working overtime and led to very sore achy bones. Because of the discomfort, he wanted to wait until my Friday blood came back before administering the shots. So back to shots in the stomach. You'd think I'd be used to that by now, but some things a person just never gets used to.

In spite of all the things I had to deal with, at one point, my biggest dilemma was how to get to work wearing both the wig and my motorcycle helmet. Regrettably, driving my car would mean having to park two blocks away, catch the light, and walk even farther. With my motorcycle, I could park next to the building.

As luck would have it, the wig took up too much space beneath my helmet. It was like wearing two hats, so I put the wig in my purse and wore just the helmet. Once I got to work, I went directly down the hall to the bathroom so that I could put on the wig. To my dismay, several people were in there lingering. I didn't know what they thought of me standing there still in my helmet while waiting for them to leave. Talk about getting weird looks. Finally, with my helmet on, I just had to walk down the hallway and go into my office. I did a quick transfer but found it difficult to position the wig in place. Not only was it a mess having been shoved into my purse, but I didn't have a mirror with an ability to see the back of my head.

Recently I was watching a television show that was sponsored by the car insurance folks who use a green gecko as their spokesperson. It occurred to me as I watched the little green fellow with his bald head, sunken chest, and protruding belly that we must be siblings, I just knew it. How else could I have that same body shape? Lest someone ask me for a rate quote on their car insurance, I'd better stay away from green outfits for the time being.

"Have I not commanded you? Be strong and of good courage; do not be afraid, nor be dismayed, for the Lord your God is with you wherever you go" (Joshua 1:9 NKJV).

October 8, 2007

Monday was a holiday for County employees, and I had registered for a class offered by the American Cancer Society and sponsored by St. Joseph's for breast cancer patients. The class was designed to teach chemo patients how to apply makeup after losing their eyebrows, eyelashes, and hair. I had visions of giant hairless babies all dolled up with makeup. Scary thought.

The plan for the day was for me to attend my "beauty" class and then meet up with Johnny and Craig for an educational conference I had registered for through Saint Joseph's. Since they were both being held in the same building, it didn't make since for me to drive all the way home and then drive back. Johnny and I agreed that I would just drive over to the nearby mall after my class ended and see about getting a wig. That should only take an hour or so; then I could drive back over to the conference center and meet up with them for the evening program.

The "Look Good, Feel Good" program turned out to be a great way to boost my confidence. The American Cancer Society provided an assortment of cosmetics and cleansers for dry "chemo" skin along with tips on how to do our makeup once we had no eyelashes to curl, eye brows to arch, or hair on our head to brush. Happily, I managed to apply a few products to my face that didn't make me look like a painted doll and then drove across the highway to the mall. As I walked around the mall, I noticed how drained I was feeling. I hadn't really done much that day, but I felt like I could barely make it from one end of the mall to the other. It took a little longer than I expected to find a wig, but after a while I was just too tired of trying them on to care. Telling the salesgirl I would wear it since I was on my way to a meeting, I paid for it and headed out to the mall exit to find my car.

When I got outside, my car wasn't there! I looked all around the lot, but it didn't seem familiar to me. Perhaps I had mistakenly gone out the wrong exit. I hadn't been to that mall before, so I retraced my steps. Looking around, I decided that I must have parked on the other side and headed in the direction of another mall exit. By the time I got out to the parking lot, I was starting to feel the fatigue really set in and started to panic. My car was nowhere in sight! Once again I scanned the parking lot, not sure of where I had left my car. On top of feeling exhausted, I was starting to feel the pressure of being late. I prided myself on never being late. This was a trait my parents had drilled into me as a child. If I told someone I would be there at a certain time, I had better be there. All of my life I was on time, if not early.

This was not like me. Not only was I frustrated that I was going to arrive late and that went against my own personal code, but this was a meeting I had really been looking forward to attending. In addition to the experts on the panel who would be discussing the latest developments in breast cancer treatments, there would be a special meeting for the kids. It was a chance for the kids to ask questions and share their feelings with someone other than their own parents. I began to feel myself losing control. Not one to cry easily, I was surprised to feel myself start to crumble. How could this be happening? Of all times, why now?

About then I got a call from Johnny. "Where are you? The meeting is about to start. Craig and I have been waiting here for over a half an hour. Are you coming?" My response must have been one that caught his attention immediately, because he quickly said, "What's wrong? What happened?"

As soon as he said that I blubbered, "I can't find my car."

"Stay there. I'll be right there. Do you know what store you are next to? Just sit down. Don't move. I'll be there to get you." Fifteen minutes later Johnny walked through the mall doors like a knight in shining armor. He wrapped his arms around me, laughed, and said, "Come on. We'll come back for your car later."

By the time we got there the room was packed. Not only were we late, but we had to go to the second row and climb over everyone to get to the only empty seats. After all the effort it took to get there, I couldn't even focus on what was being said. I was sweating, irritable, and embarrassed about arriving late. It was a disastrous evening for me. Craig, on the other hand, seemed to like his meeting. With a little bit of prodding, he told us about some of the other kids in the room and what they had shared. He did not divulge his own thoughts but agreed that it had been worth his time. I was relieved to hear him speak about it so enthusiastically. For me it was an entirely different experience. I kept these feelings to myself since I was tired, frustrated, and feeling ugly in my new ugly wig. Too bad the "Look Good, Feel Good" feeling didn't last throughout the night.

Chapter 17

MR. POTATO HEAD GETS NEW HAIR

October 11, 2007

Off to a rotten start; the steroids had to be taken again. They amped me up, kept me from sleeping, and made me feel fiery all day. Too much like menopause. On top of that I got a call from my oncologist regarding my horrible sore throat and the feeling that I was swallowing rocks. It was extreme heartburn. My doctor prescribed Prilosec to combat it. He said, "That's just another expected side effect of chemo; get used to it." This made it difficult to really eat much. In spite of that, I was already starting to take on the shape of Mr. Potato Head. It was incredible how fast I started to bloat up and gain weight.

After I saw my doctor, I went to see my friend and hairdresser, Sandy. She agreed to style my wig. I called her after I had worn it a few times and told her how I felt. I explained to her, "Each time I see myself in the mirror, I picture Harpo Marx. It's very disturbing!" The new wig I had purchased was not only expensive—it was ugly. After reading about the Susan G. Komen foundation, I decided to contact the local chapter and ask them if they had any contacts for me to get a wig. That organization is fabulous. The representative made an appointment for me to come look at the selection of wigs they had. Not only did she let me pick whatever I wanted, but she told me to choose some scarves and hats in addition to the wig. She said I wouldn't want to wear my wig all the time, because they can be very hot and itchy. Something I already knew firsthand.

So I took my two new wigs over to Sandy and asked her to make them look more like "me." She asked me how I had styled the first wig when I wore it. I told I hadn't. The box said, "Shake and go," and so that's what I did. She said, "No! Every wig needs to be styled, and most need to be cut to fit the shape of your face." No wonder it looked horrible on me. You'd think someone would have said something! I looked awful, but they were too kind to tell me!

While I was there her salon partner Richard came in and said, "Oh fun! I want to play too!" Richard pulled some wigs from a cupboard in the back and started combing them and styling them on my bald head. Long red wigs, short black, and everything in between. Meanwhile Sandy worked her magic on the two wigs I had brought in to her. It was the most fun I had experienced in a long time. They both made me feel so good about myself, and I loved them for that. As I left they reminded me about all of the recent Santa Ana winds and California fires; they advised me to stay away from both of those elements while wearing a synthetic wig. Enough said.

As I had expected, I was pretty out of it the following Monday and stayed in bed most of the day. When Craig came home from school, he came into my room looking for me. He was surprised to see me looking so haggard. The stark contrast of what he had seen just days before compared to this bloated, washed-out, foggy person I had become was surely a shock for him. The chemo cocktail I was receiving was powerful, and it was only natural that my brain felt the effects too. I certainly looked forward to being up and out of the bed soon. I knew that I felt worse than the last time, but I didn't want to think too much about that. Regrettably, I was expected to be at work in the morning, and unfortunately it was something I had requested. If I was going to make those time-off hours stretch far enough to get me through the radiation treatments, I had to be at work as many days as possible now.

Craig asked me if there was anything I needed, and I smiled and said, "Yes. Why don't you run out and get the mail? I didn't feel like going outside today."

Glad to be of some help to me, Craig ran outside to bring in the mail. He came bounding back in with a box that had been left on the front porch. He ran back to my room and exclaimed, "Hey, look, Mom! This just came for you. What do you think it is?"

Not sure what it was, I checked the label and said, "Oh, it's from Mike and Ronna up in Portland! Would you help me by opening it?"

Craig was thrilled to be able to be of assistance and even more thrilled when he opened the tall box. He said, "Wow!" as he tore back the Styrofoam peanuts and cellophane to reveal a decorated sand bucket filled with seashell cookies. Knowing that my mouth was already in pain and inflamed from the last chemo session, I told Craig to try one and tell me how they were. He eagerly agreed and dove in to the bucket. My dear friend Ronna knew how much I loved the beach, and she had just made me smile. Even though the cookies deliciously called my name, my mouth sores won that round. Nevertheless, I was content to know that she and Mike were still thinking about me. Although I didn't get to enjoy a cookie, I enjoyed something even better—a reminder that I had the best friends on the planet.

Johnny took me to chemo the next time. Once again the needle in my arm was difficult to insert, and just like the last session, it took about six hours to complete the process. Also, like the last session, I began to get a rash as soon as they plugged in the chemicals, so it was back to Benadryl and a slow drip. There was already a large red mark on my arm from the last chemo session. I feared that it threatened to become another battle scar.

Johnny stuck around about an hour and then left to go do some work. He came back around 1:30 and brought me lunch, but eating proved to be a difficult task due to my restricted diet. I had brought one of my books that Linda had brought me, a delightful mystery that I had actually been looking forward to reading. It had always been difficult for Johnny to sit still for very long, and quite frankly, I was more relaxed after he left. But I did appreciate him for taking me and picking me up, and I told him as much. He just beamed.

Chapter 18

I PLAN; THEREFORE I AM

For as long as I can remember, I have been a planner. I love to plan parties and activities, and in fact, I plan most of my life! Each year for Craig's birthday, I would start thinking and planning right after Christmas. Since he was a January baby, I would start looking for after-Christmas offers that would lend themselves to inspire a boy's birthday party. Then there was my own party, held each summer for all of my Leo friends and family. Each year was a different theme, and each attendee would be requested to wear the appropriate attire to match the theme. There were Valentine's parties, Fourth of July parties, and the most elaborate by far, our annual Christmas party! I had boxes and boxes of entertaining paraphernalia in our loft just waiting to be unpacked, polished, and presented at our holiday family-and-friend extravaganza.

This year there would be no unpacking or decorating taking place. I just didn't have it in me, and Johnny and Craig always relied on me to do it all. Other than Johnny hanging some lights and Craig decorating his own room, it was a minimalistic Christmas, and I just had to accept it. Additionally, the season was difficult for me, because not only was it clear that I wouldn't plan any big parties, but I couldn't even plan on *attending* any either. With my white cell count remaining dangerously low, I had been told by my doctor not to be out in crowds or any public places. I was nervous about shaking hands. Already I'd had to decline a few handshakes the last time we attended church and felt embarrassed in doing so.

The planner in me wanted to jump on it, get going, and make a difference. The cancer patient wanted to cry and say, "Maybe later." I knew I was experiencing the expected, but it still felt foreign and unwanted. At the same time, I had to say that if this is what I needed to go through to get what God was planning for me, then who was I to question His plans? After all, He'd been planning things longer than I had. I had a couple of great conversations with my mom and my friend Ronna regarding this frustration. They both knew me well enough to tell it like it is and keep me grounded. I really appreciated them for taking time to tell me what I needed to hear.

> "'For I know the plans I have for you,' declares the Lord, 'plans to prosper you and not harm you, and plans to give you hope and a future'" (Jeremiah 29:11 NIV).

October 22, 2007

All of a sudden my eyesight started troubling me. On top of everything else, I had a miserable UTI, compliments of all the antibiotics I had been on. What next? I was able to get in quickly to see an eye doctor. It seemed that my eyes were definitely worse than before, and I needed new glasses. Another unexpected side effect of chemo.

I received the results from the chemo lab and the blood work I had done one Friday. There were many ways to read the report, one of which was to look at the neutrophils. They should be 1.8–7.7 thou/mcl. Mine had dropped down to *.42*. That's well below the low point; thus the Cipro and the "no fresh food" warning. It seems there are too many germs on fresh fruit and vegetables that I now had no protection against. So much for any diet I'd been trying to be on. I was told too: *no dieting* during chemo. Each time I showed up to the doctor's office and weighed in, my self-esteem would be nonexistent and tears would begin to flow.

Seeing how upset I became, the nurse said to me, "Don't worry about it. It's pointless to try to lose weight while you are on the treatment. Chemo is designed to do one thing: kill cancer. Not anything else. A lot happens in your body while you are going through the treatments.

71

Just relax about it and think about getting better. You can lose the weight later."

I tearfully asked her, "What about all the *thin* cancer patients I've seen?"

"Well," she said, "they were on a different cocktail than you are."

Good grief, they get the "throw up" chemo and I get the "cupcake" chemo. Finally, I looked at her through my tears and said, "Are you sure?" She assured me and sent me on my way. I left there thinking, *That's just great. I have a chemo program that makes me hungry all the time. I have steroids in my system, and I am retaining fluids to the tune of five to eight pounds a week. To top it all off, when I do manage to eat something, I can't taste it and can barely chew because of mouth sores.* Disgruntled over the whole situation, I left there and headed for the nearest bakery.

Friday was chemo number three, and it definitely hit me harder than the previous two chemo treatments. I was wiped out over the weekend, with mouth sores (which I called corduroy mouth), extreme heartburn, fatigue, and a new addition to the list: dizziness. Additionally, I started the Neupogen shots Sunday night. Fortunately Johnny had a very steady hand and was able to administer these to me. He had learned well when he was in charge of injecting the blood thinners back in August. Neupogen is given to stimulate the bone marrow into creating more white blood cells. This is not something that went unnoticed by my body. It felt like every bone and muscle in my body had been run over, possibly by a cupcake truck. It hit me in the middle of the night, a sharp pain in my back spreading throughout the rest of my body. I wound up staying in bed and dreaming of things I would love to eat but couldn't.

The following week I started feeling a bit better. However, after Thursday's fifth injection of Neupogen, I started having the aches again. I had experienced the aches every night for four nights in a row and was used to that. What I started feeling after about three hours was totally different and scary. I started having full-blown convulsions. I had no control over my body, even though I was fully aware of my surroundings. Since I was feeling so weird, I decided to sit out on the couch for a while after Johnny went to bed. Within an hour my body was twitching and jerking beyond my control. This was like nothing I had ever experienced before. Lurching down the hall, I woke Johnny up and tried to explain my plight. It was obvious that something was wrong, and he decided that we'd better not wait for this to play out. Off to the emergency room we went.

Flying down the freeway at 12:30 in the morning, I was pulling my knees into my chest and flailing my arms about. Johnny tried to hold my hand, but I would jerk away uncontrollably. At one point I started to laugh, and he just glared at me and said, "This isn't funny!" When we got there, I was still having full-blown jerking convulsions. I felt like one of those toys we had as children where the small animal or character stands on a little platform and you push the bottom of the platform and it makes the animal collapse and then stand up again when you release the button. I was jumping all over with no ability to stop.

The staff on duty had no idea what was going on and openly stared at me as I bounced down the hall toward the exam room. Before we walked out of, or in my case *hopped* out of our front door, I had the presence of mind to grab the information about the medications I was taking. Naturally, we told them I was a cancer patient when we first arrived. During that time they took my BP—102/40 (I'm usually 90/65)—and my temperature; I had a low-grade fever. They left us in the exam room for about forty-five minutes.

At one point, tired and flustered, Johnny went out to the hall to see what was going on. He flagged down the attending nurse and said, "Do you have any idea what's going on with my wife?"

The nurse looked at him and said, "We think she's having a panic attack."

Johnny said he wanted to tell him, "You don't know my wife," but instead he came back into the exam room and told me what was said.

I gaped at him and said, "You have got to be kidding! That's their answer?"

The doctor on call finally came back in and told us that she had no idea what my problem was and that furthermore, because she had no clue, there was nothing they could do for me. Luckily the spasms started to subside about three hours after they had started. When we realized that we were getting no help from the ER team and that my condition didn't seem to be worsening, we decided to leave. After another thirty minutes when no one came back in to check on me, we both *walked* out.

The next morning when I called my oncologist, he told me that it was a side effect (not often experienced) and I should not take any more of the Neupogen injections. My own web research revealed that it was caused by an overdose of the Neupogen. I found that to be alarming since Johnny was giving me the amount prescribed by my doctor.

By the end of my ordeal, my white cell count did come up a bit, but there would not be any more boosting of my white cells after that reaction. It would have been nice to know that there was a possibility of that reaction happening so we wouldn't have been overly alarmed. Poor Johnny didn't know what to make of it. I was coherent but acting like a marionette! I knew he'd be glad when this was all over.

Chapter 19

GOING GREEN

October 26, 2007

My oncologist decided that it was not wise for me to be at work anymore. He was concerned about how low the white cell count had been and was worried that I might pick up a virus or germ and throw off my whole chemo treatment. After speaking to my boss about the doctor's orders, she agreed that that week should be my last until I was able to return after the upcoming radiation treatments were over. So I decided to go out with a bang: I made a decision to go green. Since a few people from my new office were planning to dress up for Halloween, I thought I should take advantage of an opportunity that I would hopefully never have again. I dressed as a Martian. A *green* Martian. Johnny sprayed my head and face with green face paint, and I wore a metallic silver coat. It was a very strange feeling to be walking around without hair at work. Everyone seemed to get a kick out of it, and I heard a few "you've got guts" comments. I took that as a compliment.

It was good to have a bit of fun before my last day at work. I wanted everyone to know that I was more than my hair; I was more than a cancer patient. I was my brain, character, and spirit. God designed me to withstand whatever Satan threw at me and not only live to tell about it but to laugh at it.

"Be joyful always; pray continually; give thanks in all circumstances, for this is God's will for you in Christ Jesus" (1 Thessalonians 5:16–18 NIV).

November 14, 2007

I slugged through the week, not feeling my best, but not quite bad enough to stay in bed either. Life went on, and I had to do my share. Craig's counselor at school requested a meeting to review his program for the year. Unfortunately the meeting was scheduled for 7:30 in the morning. Although I tried to explain my situation, it seemed that the school faculty had more concerns for their own record keeping and need to meet time schedules than they did for any of my personal issues. That being said, I agreed to the meeting.

At 6:30 a.m. I dragged myself out of bed and donned my most depressing cancer outfit, wrapped my head in a scarf, and made my way over to my son's middle school. After taking his first look at me, the counselor immediately expressed his appreciation to me for attending and offered his concern for my recovery. Perhaps he didn't believe me when I told him I was not really up to a meeting first thing in the morning, but judging by the look on his face, I could tell that he had become a believer.

He looked at his notes and then began: "I appreciate your coming out for this meeting. I am concerned about Craig and his homework. He's not been turning in work and seems to be sliding when it comes to participation in class."

Staring at him from under the hood of my scarf, I explained, "I have been going through chemo treatments and consequently have not been as on top of things with Craig as I would normally be. I was planning on attending open house so I could meet all of his teacher, but I didn't make it because it was on a night following my chemo treatment. His teachers probably think I don't care, but that's not true."

He assured me that that wasn't the case but agreed to make some notes about my health issues and their effects on Craig's grades. As I was leaving I assured him that I would be more diligent with asking about Craig's homework. Although it took some major effort to be there, I'm pleased I went.

November 18, 2007

For our anniversary Johnny made arrangements for us to go see *Jersey Boys*. He was able to secure two seats that were relatively alone, with no one sitting on either side of us. If that weren't the case, I don't think I would have been able to go, not with my white cell count being so low. I was itching to get out of the house, so I ventured over to the mall to get Johnny a card and a little anniversary present. This time I was smart: I went to the mall I usually went to and made a note of where I parked my car. By the time I got from my car to the store, shopped, got back to the car, and drove home, I was definitely feeling the effects of the drugs in my system. It had been five months prior that I had first experienced the "shop-till-you-drop" phenomenon.

We had a lovely time at the theater, and we relaxed a bit. It had been quite a while since we had gone anywhere or done anything that didn't have to do with cancer. Later that night as I was reflecting on our evening, I had to admit that Johnny had been trying to be more available and support the things I needed him to do. Just taking care of the things around the house helped me so much and relieved much of the tension for me. With him never having been the kind of guy who handles illness or unpleasantness very well, I recognized that this whole cancer thing was a stretch for him. Perhaps that was why when people called to ask about me, I would hear him saying, "She's great!" At first I wasn't sure if he really believed that or if he just didn't want our friends to worry. It made more sense to me when I thought about his personality and how he navigated his own life. It took a lot to get Johnny down. Like many men, he didn't say much when something was bothering him, so I would always have to figure it out, usually long after the event had taken place. To compound his perplexity of my plight, in his opinion this was a "woman's issue," and far be it for him to try to understand.

As I sat on the bed and thought about all of this, he came in to the bedroom and leaned over to kiss me and said, "I had a nice time with you tonight. Happy anniversary."

I kissed him back and said, "I had a fabulous time. Thank you for making it happen. Happy anniversary, Johnny."

At that point we both wriggled into our designated side of the bed and went to sleep. There would be no cuddling, no further kissing, and certainly no sex. Not that I expected it. I couldn't very well expect my husband to be interested in my body when I wasn't ready to accept it either. Nothing had prepared me for the reality of what *exactly* would be lost when I had a double mastectomy. Obviously I would look different, but it all hit home now that there would never be any feeling in my breast area again, I would never feel my husband caress me and be able to respond in the way I once had. There was so much more to the loss of my breasts than just what I looked like without them, and I wasn't sure how long it would take me or *us* to move past it. Little did I know then, but it would take *years*.

Chapter 20

GIVE THANKS ... AND PASS THE CHEMO

November 22, 2007

Staring at the turkey in front of me, I already knew that it wasn't going to taste like any Thanksgiving bird I had eaten in the past. Cranberry sauce was out of the question because of the high acidic factor, and stuffing, well, that could have been sawdust for all I knew. No offense to my mom—she is an award-winning southern cook—but chemo had done a number on me, and I was not going to remember Thanksgiving because of the meal. Instead, I discovered so many other things to be thankful for, things that in the past I had most likely taken for granted. I began to look forward to having a drink of water that didn't leave a metallic taste in my mouth. Likewise, being able to eat without extreme heartburn or irritating the sores in my mouth would be such a pleasure. Although I had been on antibiotics for the past two months, I thankfully had not gotten another UTI. Additionally, I had to be thankful for having the time off from work (with pay) to fight my illness. I was also thanking God for the multitude of prayers, well wishes, and positive thoughts so many people sent my way. Yes, I was indeed thankful.

Well, more blood work and then I would start the last dose of steroids for my last round of chemo. That last round would prove to be the most difficult round due to my white cell count dropping to almost nonexistent. Since my bad reaction and trip to the ER because of the Nupogen, my oncologist told me that I could not rely on that treatment for help. Unfortunately there was nothing I could do to help improve the situation; the blood cells would do whatever they chose to do. However, I *could* control the amount of germs I came into contact with. We had hand sanitizer containers all over the house, we bought a new Rainbow vacuum system that actually purified the air as the water circulated through the canister, and ultimately, Johnny had to tell some friends of ours not to come over to the house. They were in town and really wanted to visit. Johnny asked them if any of their kids were sick. When they told him that their one child had a cold, Johnny kindly told them that unfortunately they could not come for a visit. Hearing him say that I changed my mind about his understanding of how I was doing. I realized that he did get it but just didn't show it in an outwardly way many times.

The day after Thanksgiving was my last chemo, and my childhood friend Cathy was my companion for the day. Although she lived an hour away, she had been calling regularly and offering to help. However, she hadn't said anything about wanting to go to one of my chemo appointments. Out of respect I didn't say anything to her, because I knew it might be tough for her. She had lost her mom to cancer a few years earlier, and I certainly didn't want her to think that she had to be there with me, especially if it meant revisiting those difficult times. When Cathy finally said she wanted to be there with me, I happily accepted her offer and made plans for her to pick me up and go with me.

The last treatment was no different in that it took the full six hours. I had my predictable allergic reaction, and my body began to heat up immediately. What made that last treatment different than the first was that by that time my veins were shot. Disappointingly, like some patients are able to, I was not allowed to have a "port" inserted into my chest. A port is used to connect you to the IV tubes that deliver the medication for each chemotherapy session. The port remains in place for the duration of your treatments. To this day, my eyes can still spot a "port scar" on another woman, and my heart goes out to her.

In my case, I was told that because I was going to receive radiation and because I had a very minimal area of usable flesh I would have to endure the needles each time. That last time the nurse had a very difficult time finding a vein for that very large needle. At first I was squirming around, feeling the pain but not making any noise. But finally the needles proved to be too much, and I let out a howl. It was just too much, and I started to shed tears. Once the nurse got the needle in place and moved away, I noticed that Cathy was on the far side of the room. She saw me looking at her and came back over to where I was situated in my recliner. We didn't talk about it then, but later that night Cathy confided in me, "I am so sorry I walked away when the nurse was trying to find your vein today; I just couldn't stand to see you in pain like that."

I told her, "I knew it might be difficult for you today. Don't give it another thought. Besides, the worst of it is over. I'm *done* with chemo!"

Although I was not happy about where I was with the state of my health, I was alive, and that was the foremost goal for the time being. In time I hoped I would start to look like a woman again, have new hair, and lose the extra thirty-five pounds of weight that I was hauling around. I was thankful that I had a few weeks to get strong and ready myself for the radiation treatments.

That night as I prepared myself for bed, I prayed, "Dear God, just so you know, I'm thankful to have the sweet friends in my life that make this so much more bearable. I am also thankful to have my son and husband with me during this difficult time. Thank you for keeping my parents strong. I am thankful for them too. I don't know that I would have held up as well as they have if it was Craig going through cancer. Yet, they have been constantly cheerful, helpful, and loving."

> "Oh, give thanks to the Lord, for He is good! For
> His mercy endures forever" (Psalms 136:1 AKJV).

November 29, 2007

I went back on Cipro again. No salad, fresh fruit, vegetables, or anything that hadn't been cooked. The antibiotics had to be taken for ten days. I had been on those wretched things for more than two full months. One would think my body would have been immune to them by then.

Not surprisingly I had a tough time with the last chemo and was in bed for a couple of days. Looking back on that month I realize that there would have been no way I could have gone to work even if my white blood cell count wasn't too low.

Even though I wasn't at work anymore, I continued to receive the nicest cards and e-mails from my coworkers as well as other friends. Out of the blue I received a lovely card and gift from a group of friends we didn't see very often. They are a group of people who own Vespas, and we enjoyed meeting up with them occasionally for long rides. We also enjoyed trips to Santa Barbara, Solvang, and even long trips to San Diego. Because our Vespa community was tightly knit and kept in touch with each other, many of our fellow riders knew of my illness. Several of them were getting my updates and e-mails and were aware of where I was with my treatment program. Generously, a group of them pitched in and purchased a two-hundred-dollar gift card from a healthy gourmet online food delivery service. That gift would prove to be especially helpful when I began my radiation treatments. Johnny and Craig could choose what they wanted to eat for the week, and it would be delivered to the house. All they needed to do was heat it up. That two hundred dollars would feed them for a month! What a thoughtful and beneficial gift that turned out to be. It's so easy to put people out of mind when they are out of sight. I'm so thankful that our friends didn't do that. One particular friend from that same group called me every few days just to tell me a joke. Mike, a funny, great big, tattooed guy twenty years my junior, warmed my heart and blessed my soul with laughter. He taught me to never underestimate whom God could use in my life.

December 4, 2007

For over a week I rarely left my bed. I trudged to the bathroom or to get something to drink. Other than that, I saw no reason to hoist myself from the security of my bed. My body was wiped out, and it finally crashed and seemed to say, "No more!" Unfortunately, an appointment with the oncologist required me to get up, get dressed, and get out of the house, none of which I felt up to doing.

There was this little "cord" feeling under the skin near my right armpit. When the doctor checked it, he said, "I think you have another small blood clot, probably from your surgery. Don't worry; it will probably dissipate soon enough. After all, you are still taking the blood thinners."

Then he motioned for me to get on the scale. Slowly I made my way over to the hateful torture device. This was cruelty! Why was it necessary to weigh me each time I came to his office? It was just more of the same, pound upon pound of extra weight. No wonder I didn't want to get out of bed. Tears streamed down my face. He saw the look on my face and said gently, "It's just chemo and steroids; not normal weight gain. Your metabolism is next to zero while on these treatments. You'll see; you will drop the water weight and return to normal soon."

He and his nurse were both telling me that they saw it all the time and that there was no use in trying to get rid of it right now because I'd just be frustrated. Of course I was frustrated; this was the same sermon they had given me the last time I was there. Their words didn't make a difference in the way I felt about myself at that point. Not only was my chest concave after having my breasts removed, but I was completely hairless and had now packed on an extra forty pounds! I loathed the sight of myself: I looked like a bald, middle-aged, overweight *man*. With every chemo treatment I gained between six and eight pounds! I needed to calm down. I had to get focused on what I was doing and remember that this was only a process, and the process wasn't over yet. It was possibly one of the worst parts of the process, but I knew that it was always darkest before the light. This just couldn't last forever. By the time I got to my car, I was already thinking about what good I could get from this predicament. Besides the obvious, I realized that I had *no wrinkles*. My wrinkles had been completely plumped up, giving me completely smooth skin. No Botox needed. I was right in style, even if I did look like the Pillsbury Doughboy.

Chapter 21

'TIS THE SEASON

After many weeks of not being allowed to eat anything uncooked, I was finally given the go-ahead to enjoy a salad. Many supplements had been added to my diet in the hopes of boosting the alarmingly low white blood cell count. At one point it was down to .03! While I was going through chemo, I was told that I should not try to build my system up. Apparently it would interfere with the killing of the cancer cells. It sounds ridiculous, but I obliged.

After a few weeks of rebuilding I would be leaving for Los Angeles, where I would undergo six weeks of radiation. Rather than go back and forth, I would be staying in a small apartment in Hollywood. It would come to be known as my "radiation vacation." Since I would be living alone for those forty days and forty nights, I would take the time to de-stress, eat healthy, get out for some fresh air, and treat myself to some uninterrupted "me" time. Although I had misgivings about being away from Craig for so long, I was still actually looking forward it. Ultimately, this was much better than running back and forth to the radiation facility and spending so much time on the road.

Immediately following radiation, I would begin my adjuvant treatment of Tamoxifan. Additionally, I would need to remain on the blood thinners for several months until my body adjusted and the doctor was sure the two blood clots had dissipated. My oncologist also said that in approximately 75 percent of his breast cancer patients the woman would begin menopause during chemo. Since I seemed to already be showing many if not most of the symptoms, he told me that he would replace the

Tamoxifan with a different drug to accommodate the lack of hormones in my system. Tamoxafin has estrogen blockers in addition to the cancer-fighting properties. If I didn't need to block the estrogen, then I would be placed on a different, more focused drug, like Femara. Whichever drug I wound up on, I would be expected to take it for five years.

December 7, 2007

I tried to be really careful to avoid germs, going through bottles of Purell, wearing gloves when I was in public, and staying out of crowds and most public areas. It startled me to realize how many things people touch that were touched by numerous others—elevator buttons, water fountains, doors, pens, and keypads at the checkout, the arms of the chair at the movie theater, railings on the staircase … the list goes on and on. Furthermore, I felt guilty that we hadn't been to church in such a long time, but it was just too crowded. It also bothered me to withdraw my hand when people plunged their hand at me to shake. They would get the oddest look on their face. Then I would feel like I had to go into a whole explanation. It's just wasn't worth it.

December 13, 2007

Finally I was able to get out and see a few friends. Not able to get out before this, I relied on the wonderful world of Amazon to supply me with the gifts I would be needing. Actually, I had a lot of fun doing that and would consider doing all of my shopping that way in the future! As I made my way out to visit some friends and distribute a few of the gifts I had purchased, they greeted me with gentle hugs and remarks about how great I looked. Perhaps that was because I didn't have the thin, drawn look that people consider when they think of cancer. Although I didn't feel like myself and certainly didn't like looking at myself in the mirror, I accepted their compliments with gratitude. It was certainly better than telling me I looked like the Pillsbury Doughboy, which was more accurate. In this case I appreciated my friends not stating the bold truth!

Speaking of the Pillsbury Doughboy, even though none of my clothes fit, I refused to go out and buy a whole new wardrobe. Instead, I borrowed a few of Johnny's more brightly colored button-up shirts. I was able to throw one on over my little pink mastectomy camisole and add jewelry.

However, the one thing I did have to go out and purchase was a pair of really nice black leisure/sweat pants. They were a staple of my "new" wardrobe, and I couldn't live without them. While shopping for the black ones I found a pair of red ones on sale and thought, *What the heck? It's Christmas time; it'll be festive.* What I didn't think about was how anything in red stands out so much more. And although I would have gotten away with wearing it in my former, much smaller size, it looked entirely different at my new plus size. Since I was only five foot one, forty pounds was enough to bump me up five sizes. One afternoon after doing some light grocery shopping, I was getting into my car and some unthinking person made a remark that still stings. They shouted out, "Hey, Santa, where's your sleigh?" Perhaps I had it coming by wearing a "Santa" hat instead of my wig in conjunction with the red sweats.

December 15, 2007

It felt as if I were carrying around giant bags of dog food everywhere I went. The simplest of tasks or activities would have me winded and exhausted in a matter of minutes. This was a foreign feeling to me. All of my life people had told me how energetic I was and how they could not keep up with me. Before cancer, I actually took satisfaction in being able to outlast most of my friends in the stamina and energy department. So when Craig had a doctor's appointment, I felt that it was necessary for me to gear up and take him. Although the doctor was surprised to see me, I assured him that this was important to me and I wanted to be there. My other reason for attempting to go to any appointments that involved Craig was that I felt that it was necessary for me to show Craig that I wasn't going to let cancer get me down or keep me from being his mom. The reality was that it had been a long five months and it wasn't over yet, but I wasn't ready to let it get the best of me.

Middle school is not an easy time for most kids, and it certainly wasn't for Craig. He wasn't always open about how he felt, and I knew that he had been afraid of losing me. Because of my awareness of his fears, I made sure that when I was feeling discouraged or depressed I didn't show it in front of him. Many a shower was taken with the distinct purpose of shedding tears as opposed to washing my body. The shower was the one place in my home where I could go to and no one would bother me, check on me, or disturb my privacy.

Chapter 22

THE GRINCH THAT TRIED TO STEAL CHRISTMAS

December 21, 2007

I had an ultrasound done, and the technician said that my veins looked clear. He traveled up and down the arm and couldn't see any clotting. Hallelujah! Praise God for that. My oncologist kept me on the blood thinners for the next few weeks just as a precaution. I had been experiencing numbness in both of my hands. I would wake up several times during the night with no feeling in my fingers and arms, and at first I thought, *Oh no, not another blood clot*, but my doctor said that it was the effect of the Taxadrine drug I received during chemo. The neuropathy is common and might take years to go away, if ever.

The difficulty in getting around was due to the soreness and stiffness in my bones. I felt like I had performed an intense workout and because of it could barely lift myself out of a chair. According to my research, this pain could be a response to my bone marrow making more white cells and should eventually ease up. My cell count was under 150 (up from .03), but it was supposed to be above 500. It was working its way up; I could literally feel it!

Although my spirits were down, I continued to receive God's grace and compassion. A huge blessing came my way: I received additional catastrophic leave donations from my friends at the County. Remarkably, I received exactly enough time to be off for my radiation treatments. Eight weeks was what I needed, and that was exactly what the hours totaled up to be! Just as the Israelites received their daily portion of manna—just what was needed, no more, no less—I too had received my gracious portion. God certainly put it on the heart of each of my supporters to donate exactly what they felt comfortable giving, which of course was exactly what I needed. Truly a miraculous Christmas gift.

December 31, 2007

In preparation for the upcoming radiation I was soon to receive, I got a phone call from the oncologist-radiologist. The doctor said as I answered the phone, "Good afternoon, Tammy. I just wanted to remind you that your radiation will begin in January. Because of your unusual situation you will be having your entire left chest wall radiated." Again that word "unusual." He went on to say, "We typically radiate the exact point on the chest where the tumor was found. In your unusual case, however, we don't know where the 'ghost' tumor was. So just to be sure all of the microscopic pieces have been dealt with, we will radiate the entire left chest wall."

Once again I was listening to the words but thinking about something else. This whole procedure would have a huge impact on whether I would be able to have reconstructive surgery later. I already knew the outcome of this massive radiation: the skin would be damaged, become very tough, and lose its elasticity, thus making reconstruction a remote possibility. I was brought back to the conversation when the oncologist said, "So remember, you will need to have very soft T-shirts and comfortable clothes to wear during those six weeks. Absolutely no deodorant or harsh soaps of any kind. You will receive a list of approved items when you get up to the radiation center. If you have any questions after that, you can call my office. We'll see you in January. Happy Holidays."

Looking back on the year I could only think, *Never say never.* Incredibly, something I *never* thought would happen to me suddenly consumed my life. I remembered looking at the statistics for breast cancer in a magazine—"One out of eight women will get breast cancer"—and thinking, *Hmm, I wonder which of the women I work with will be that statistic?* Never in a million years did I expect it to be me. I was the health nut, the one who took all the supplements. I didn't smoke, drink, or even drink soda. It just made me realize how one never knows what's around the corner or what we will be challenged to overcome. One of my favorite scriptures was now my mantra: "I can do all things in Christ, who strengthens me" (Philippians 4:13 KJV).

Chapter 23

LIVING IN LA AND GETTING TATTOOS

January 2008

Radiation itself was a breeze compared to the process of actually getting into my new little apartment. Car problems on the way put me off course and late for my first appointment, the one appointment I was warned not to be late to! Finding the facility on Sunset Boulevard was not easy either. There were about seven huge healthcare facilities up and down Sunset Boulevard. Naturally I went to the wrong one the first time and then couldn't find parking once I found the actual building. I wound up valet parking just so I could get to the appointment. The valet gave me a strange look when I pulled up in a panic with my little car stuffed to the top with all my supplies for the next six weeks.

After the appointment I went to check into my apartment. The street my apartment was on was under construction, and both ends of the street had been blocked off. After circling the block several times, I spotted an alley, drove down it, and plunged onto the torn-up street. Inching my way across the ragged asphalt, I spotted the driveway of the apartments. Parking in the driveway, I wearily climbed the stairs only to find a sign on the door: "Out to lunch." I stood there looking around for a while. After not seeing anyone, I went back to my car and sat in the driver's seat. As long as no one tried to pull in to the driveway, I would be okay.

After a while two women walked up the stairs to the locked front door. When they started to go in, I jumped out of my car and said,

"Hi there! I'm a new tenant and I was wondering how I get into the building."

As they turned to me, I was surprised to see that one of them looked pregnant. The other woman looked slightly older, so I thought perhaps she was the girl's mother. The older woman called over to me, "Oh, we can let you in. Just wait there and I'll go around and push the button."

As the security gate began to rise, I slowly drove my car into the underground parking structure and parked in an empty stall. As soon as I opened my door, they walked up to me and said, "Hi!"

I was grateful for their help and said, "Thank you so much. I didn't know what to do when the street was under construction, and then the door was locked, so I am so thankful you showed up when you did."

The pregnant one introduced herself: "I'm Wendy, and this is my mom. Will you be staying here?"

I smiled and introduced myself and then said, "Yes. I'm not sure what to do. I have a bunch of stuff with me, and I'm hoping there's a cart or something I can use to transport it to my apartment. When do you think the manager will return?"

They assured me that she would return soon and that if I just sat in the chair outside her door she would be able to assist me. In about ten minutes the apartment manager did return and promptly told me that there were no carts available; they had been locked up for the day. She went on to inform me that the elevators were being worked on and I'd have to use the stairs if I wanted to get into my apartment right away. I must have looked at her a little feebly as I said, "What floor is my apartment on?" She glanced at her desk and pulled a folder and a key out of a file sorter. The arrangements had already been made by my doctor, so I didn't need to sign anything or provide her with any information other than my name.

She looked up at me and said, "You are going to be on the fourth floor." After another glance at her paperwork, she said, "Come on. Let's see if I can find you a cart."

I wasn't sure what I was supposed to do with a cart if I was expected to walk up four flights of stairs, but I trailed down the hall after her. At the end of the hall there was a locked storage room. She pulled out a key and put it in the lock, and the door opened. *Voila*—there were three carts behind the door just waiting for someone to use. Surprised by that, I wasn't sure what to make of it. I wished my two new friends were still hanging around so I could ask them if this was a common practice or was I just being given the runaround. Since they had already made their way up the stairs to their own apartment, I had no one to ask about the elevator situation other than the woman who had just unlocked the door. I hesitated and then decided that I had nothing to lose by asking, "When do you think the elevator will be working again? I'd hate to load up one of these carts and then not be able to take it up to my apartment. I don't want to inconvenience you again."

She told me to take a cart, and as she closed and locked the door again she said, "Wait here." In a few minutes she came back and motioned for me to follow her once again.

As we rounded the corner, an elevator repairman walked toward us and said, "It's all good. The elevator is working again."

Not sure if this was normal or not, I didn't stop to ask her anything else. I rolled the cart out to my car and began the enormous task of unloading it. Since I was going to be there for six weeks, I had quite an assortment of what I considered necessary items: my laptop, George Foreman cooker, several books, writing materials, camera, CDs, iPod, docking station, electronic chargers, a few kitchen spices, vitamins, medication, several bottles of seltzer water, a couple of pairs of shoes, the required T-shirts, and my ever-present sweat pants. All that and my personal toiletries made for a carload of gear. After three trips to the car and back, I was finally ready to return the cart. Once again she was nowhere to be found. I left the cart next to the locked door and made a mental note to go back to the office in an hour or so and let her know I had returned it. What an ordeal. I hoped that it was not a hint of what was in store for me over the next forty days and forty nights in Hollywood.

After I settled into my little apartment, I called Johnny to let him know that I had arrived. He had begun to wonder, since it had been hours since I had left our house in Irvine. I said, "It's very nice, and I have a living room with a TV, a small bedroom, and a little bathroom. The kitchen is tiny, but it's all one person really needs. Perhaps you and Craig can come up next weekend and see it in person." He told me that they would try and that Craig and he had just put their food in to cook and it was ready. I told him to let me know how the food selection was since he was in charge of using the gift card for them to eat while I was in Hollywood. After I hung up I felt a little sad, but I needed to get unpacked and so focused on that and then went to bed.

The next morning I was scheduled to be at the radiation facility for my instructions and "markings." I didn't know what that meant, but I was curious and felt that I might be in for a surprise. Once I checked in with Mark the receptionist, I was called back into the radiation room. The technicians there were all very friendly and engaging.

One particularly sociable technician took me into the actual room where my radiation would take place and began to tell me what to expect. "This is the actual machine that we will use. Because the rays are so strong, we are in the room over there (he pointed), behind an iron and cement wall. We try to have you come to the same room each time. It makes it easier for you to remember, and before you come in, go down the hall to the scale (he pointed again) and weigh in. Oh, speaking of that, we don't want you to lose any weight during your treatments. It makes it too difficult for us to line up your markers with our laser beams." I must have had a questioning look on my face, because he continued on, "So many women who are going through radiation right after chemo try to lose the weight they've gained. I'm just telling you; it's not recommended. If you do lose weight and we can't line you up because you've lost body mass, you'll have to be re-marked."

I said, "What's that? What's the marking system you're talking about?"

He turned and smiled at me and said, "That's next. Follow me. You're going to see a man about some tattoos. Welcome to Hollywood!"

Down the hall in a small office I met the man who would once again remind me to "never say never." He explained to me that each day the tattoos I was about to be given would serve as a guide for the laser beams. When I arrived for my daily treatment, I would be positioned on the table, and then the technician could easily and accurately line up my body with the tattoos, allowing for a perfectly placed dose of radiation. He told me that "back in the day" they used permanent markers to mark the skin. But over time they would get smudged and rub off, thus compromising accuracy. Therefore, I would receive four *permanent* tattoos: one in the middle of my breast bone, one under my left arm, one under my left rib, and another just under my collarbone. Of course I didn't have any say in the design of my tattoos; otherwise I might have requested a couple of seashells. Never having acquired any tattoos before, I was feeling rather apprehensive. However, there really wasn't anything to get disturbed over; as it turned out all four tattoos were small and look like little blue freckles.

Radiation began the next afternoon at 3:30. The radiation itself was not difficult or painful. That being said, the machine was a huge intimidating monster with arms that rotated about while filling the air with clanging, banging, and whistling. During the procedure I was required to remain motionless for eight minutes to allow the machine to properly work its magic. Most of the time when I arrived the technicians had extremely loud music playing in an attempt to overshadow the racket of the machine. Overall, the whole experience was rather surreal.

Although I had been warned to not lose too much weight, I had been given the go-ahead to eat healthy, go on walks, and try to regain as much stamina as I wanted to. Even though my goal was to lose as much of the chemo weight as possible, I was really interested in just feeling better and stronger. My circulation had been a big concern. For over a week, my arms kept going numb during the night. I would wake up several times during the night with both arms and hands completely numb. Even though I was told that was a common side effect of the chemo, I was under the impression that it would be just my hands and not my arms too. During the day I found myself constantly flexing my hands to get rid of the tingling, but once I went to bed at night I was awakened by the pulsing of my lifeless limbs. It was a scary feeling, yet no one seemed to be as concerned as I was.

January 15, 2008

After a full week in Hollywood, I started to feel at home. It had been a good break from the stress of managing a home while dealing with cancer. At the Kenmore Apartments, everyone was in the same boat. The surrounding buildings were mostly hospital facilities, and the residents of the neighborhood were used to seeing patients. That made for an unusual and yet oddly relaxing situation.

It took a whole week, but I finally I saw one of the women who had let me in to the parking structure that first nerve-racking day. Although I had met Wendy that first day, it was the first time we had a chance to talk and share our stories. Still curious to know if she really was pregnant, I approached her and said, "Hello again. Wendy, right?"

She looked up and smiled and said, "Hi. You look like you got all settled in. That was a rough day for you, huh?"

I laughed and said, "Yes. I'm so glad you and your mom were there to help me. Is your mom still here?"

She said, "No. She only comes for a couple of days during the week. Then she has to get back to help with my kids." As she spoke she lit a cigarette. Shock must have shown on my face, because she quickly took a puff and then said, "Oh, my doctor knows that I smoke. He told me I had so much on my plate that he didn't expect me to quit smoking too. I am doing the best I can with four small children and a husband who doesn't even want me to be here."

Shocked at her revelation, I said, "Oh, no, bless your heart! How long are you scheduled to be here?"

As she took another puff and tried to blow the smoke downwind of my face, she said, "I'm not sure. The doctor said this is the last thing we can do for my ovarian cancer. I've already done a round of chemo, and that's why my husband wants me to just come home and be with him and the kids. But the doctor wanted to try this chemo-radiation combo. I hate it, but I've got four kids so I've got to try." She stepped on the cigarette butt and said, "Just look at me. I'm so bloated, and yet I'm sick to my stomach all the time, and so I can't even eat. I don't know what I'm going to do. I may just try to drive back and forth each day for the treatments. We live in Lancaster. It's about a ninety-minute drive, but at least I could be there at night to help with the kids."

I tried to think of something comforting to say, but I was at a loss for words. Instead I said, "I'm in apartment 403. Anytime you want to come by and just talk, I would love it. At the very least come by and say good-bye before you move out, if that's what you decide to do."

I wasn't sure what else to say to this poor sweet girl. She was so young and so sick. My heart broke for Wendy.

Chapter 24

PICK YOUR POISON: RADIATION OR RAISING A TEENAGER

January 23, 2008

It was the day of my son's birthday, and I had just become a mother of a teenager. I presumed that having teenagers was the thing every parent dreaded. Perhaps my view on things had been altered due to the experiences I had been having over the previous six months. However, I still felt blessed to have a son, whether he was a teenager, a toddler, or a grown man. Hopefully he would become stronger, compassionate, and more aware because of my ordeal.

Driving back to Orange County for my son's celebration, I reflected on the upcoming appointment with the neurologist on Monday. Although I had an appointment on the previous Friday, the doctor had cancelled it one hour before I was supposed to be there. So as it turned out, I would be able to see the doctor on Monday before driving back to LA for my daily radiation. The MRI took forty-five minutes. Compared to my daily radiation treatments, it was grueling. After being in the tube for twenty minutes, I was rolled out, a huge needle was jammed into my hand, an entire tube of contrast was emptied into me, and I was thrust back into the tube for another twenty-five minutes. Can you say "Cornish game hen"? The ultimate findings of the whole ordeal was nothing more than the discovery of a small amount of arthritis in my neck.

That entire weekend was stressful for me. Being back home again was a challenge, even if it was for a celebration. I recognized that in my absence there were numerous things that were not getting done. It was a struggle for me to not address them, but I didn't want my two days at home to be filled with resentment or hurt feelings. The time at home was spent on things like grocery shopping, cooking, and doing dishes. I did get a chance to go for a long walk with my friend Norma. She was excited to see me and see how my hair growth was coming along. The last time she saw me I was still sporting the shaved look she had given me six months earlier. Before I left on Monday I went through the mail, laundered a few towels and sheets, and vacuumed. As I walked out the door I said, "Tiki, you're on your own. Take care of the guys for me."

Relieved to be back on my radiation vacation, I walked all the way down to Paramount Studios the next day. The studio was on strike, so there were people with picket signs and reporters and tourists everywhere. People were all around me. A month earlier I would have been nervous to be in such a crowd. But on that day I just powered through like I belonged there. My legs were tired when I got back to the apartment, but I felt good for having just completed a six-mile walk. As I came through the front lobby, the apartment manager flagged me down. "You have mail today, and a couple of packages I signed for," she said. I was delighted to hear that and went in to her office to claim the packages. As I was looking at the largest box to see who had sent it, she said, "You sure get a lot of mail and visitors. What do you do to have all these friends? Are you famous or something?"

I looked up at her and smiled and said, "No, just blessed."

One of the packages came from my dear friend Claire. She sent me the sweetest Valentine's card and a beautiful new blouse. She was always so thoughtful. The blouse was made from a luxurious cotton and was extremely roomy, so it just barely skimmed my body; it felt splendid. Although Claire and I had been friends since the eighties we didn't get to see each other more than a couple of times a year. But she utilized the postal service to express her love every now and then, making sure I knew she was thinking of me. If that weren't already lifting my spirits, the second package was from a couple of our Vespa friends. They thoughtfully sent a huge box of goodies including a custom-designed shirt. Knowing that Johnny and I were *Survivor* fans, Nyle had used a *Survivor*-style logo, and the wording on the shirt said, "Outsmart, Outlast, Outlive; It's Reality, Not TV. CANCER SURVIVOR." Along with the shirt, his wife Connie had included a sweet Valentine's card and some little treats. They were both so very kind and thoughtful, and it was just the pick-me-up I needed.

The second half of my radiation had begun, and during the fourth week I felt the effects on the outside of my skin. The skin on the left side of my chest was red. The area where they put the pad on me before the machine began was a perfect square of red. The pad was supposed to diffuse the rays more evenly across my chest. It must have been working, because it was red and a bit itchy in one area. I wound up sleeping a bit later. I don't know if that was due to the radiation or if I was coming down with something. It was so hard to know when I was feeling the effects of chemo too.

My goal was to do something relaxing each day and still be back daily for my 3:30 appointment with the radiation department. In addition to that, I wanted to have something fun to look forward to each week. So to help me accomplish that goal, I was paid a visit by my dear friend Linda. We had a good time checking out the Hollywood/LA area and then enjoyed lunch at a landmark diner. It was so nice to actually be able to taste something again.

I continued to walk every day, more and more each day. One day I walked up a very steep street, checking my pulse a couple of times as I huffed along. It seemed to be where it should be, so I kept going. My healthy diet seemed to be helping too. When I hopped on the technician's scale, it registered another two pounds lost since Monday when I had weighed last. Although I was delighted, I knew that I had to not lose too much or the technicians would be giving me a lecture.

My only real concern and anxiety was about my son. He wasn't doing or turning in his homework. Realizing that there was only so much I could do from LA, I sent a long letter to his counselor at school. I was hoping that she could assist me in keeping him on track in making sure he was getting his homework done. I pleaded with her to please help me since I would be in LA continuing my radiation treatments for another three weeks. I also looked at his class records on line to see what was going on in each class, even if I couldn't change what had already been done. I also had another long phone conversation with him. Of course he always promised and said he was sorry, but there was no guarantee that anything was going to change until I returned home. Johnny was just not a rule enforcer; he was the "fun" parent, and Craig knew it.

Wendy finally came to see me. She knocked on my door, and as I opened it she said, "You told me to come by if I wanted to talk and to say good-bye, so here I am."

I was delighted to see her. I had been thinking about her often and had added her to my prayers each night. I welcomed her with a hug and said, "What's new with you? You look better tonight than the last time I saw you. Is that because you are doing better?"

She frowned and said, "Unfortunately it's not good news. My doctor told me after this last round of radiation that they want to do internal radiation. Apparently this tumor is inoperable. Initially they told me they would remove the tumor; now they are telling me another story. My mom agrees that I should just go home. Because I'm having so many complications and severe problems, I'm just not sure it's worth it."

I was speechless, feeling like nothing I could say would be enough to comfort her in this very serious situation. So I reached for her hand and said, "Would it be okay if we prayed together?" I asked her not knowing if she was a Christian or even believed in God, but I felt that this young women needed any kind of elevating, encouragement, and blessing she could get.

After I prayed with her, we continued to talk. I asked her about getting second opinions and any other options that she might have. I reminded her that the Internet was always a good place just to get ideas that could be researched further and even discussed with a doctor. It concerned me that was she was obviously exhausted, scared, and about to give up. It was all I could do to not cry in front of her. I had been blessed with so many people supporting me and my decisions. My treatments were straightforward and bearable, and ultimately I had a gleaming light at the end of my tunnel. She on the other hand was going through hell and had no idea if it was even going to help her. It started to get late, and I could see that she was fading. As I walked her to the door, I pressed a note with my address on it into her hand and then reached out to hug her. She accepted my embrace and said how much she appreciated our talk and how happy she was that we had met.

After a few days of not seeing her around the building, I decided to ask the radiation techs about her. They knew everyone and knew right away who I was asking about. "No, we haven't seen her in quite a while," they said. That same afternoon I made a point of finding the apartment manager and asked her if she knew what happened to Wendy. "Nope, haven't seen her. I guess her time was up." Although I knew that what she meant was Wendy's treatments had probably ended and so it was "time" for her to move out, I still cringed when she said it. But the ugly truth was that she was right. Sadly, I never heard from Wendy again.

My radiation vacation was drawing to an end. Twelve more treatments and I would be going home. I continued to use the time as a health retreat. Determined, I continued to walk at least two miles every day. Feeling especially energetic one day, I walked up to the Griffith Park Observatory. Although it was only a few miles, it was a steep incline the whole way and I wasn't sure I'd make it. Nonetheless I just trudged along. When I finally reached the top, as a reward for my herculean efforts I decided to go in to the observatory. The last time I had been inside was as a child when my class had gone there on a field trip. It brought back lovely memories. It was enchanting, and I was struck by the beauty of things so far beyond our world, things we give no thought to until they are brought to our attention, much like my own journey; I had given no thought to breast cancer until it was placed squarely into view.

My chest was beyond red, almost maroon. It was also unbearably prickly and itchy. The burned area was about the size of a paper towel. When I saw the doctor, he said that my treatment area actually looked good compared to many people. He said that the first couple of weeks of treatment didn't really show until you'd been there a few weeks. Then those first two weeks show up, and from then on it was a cumulative effect. Similarly, the last few weeks show up even after the radiation treatments are over, continuing to build upon the previous treatments. The burned area would continue to get worse even after the treatments ended.

February 4, 2008

Just when I was starting to feel down, I had a visit from one of my funniest friends. My work buddy Brandi came to visit and had me smiling and laughing the whole time. She had a way of telling even the most mundane story so that everyone laughed. She was a true entertainer, and I loved spending time with her. It was great that she came to see me, because the rest of the day was not great.

After Brandi left, I walked down to get my radiation. When I returned to my apartment, I fired up the computer to check e-mails. One of the first e-mails I received was from Craig's school. It was his report card. Aghast, I tried calling him. No one answered his phone, the house phone, Johnny's work phone, or Johnny's cell phone. Not knowing what to think, I went on to the other e-mail and decided to try again later. Around 6:00 I tried calling again, and in the middle of my leaving another message on the house phone, Craig finally answered. I told him I wanted to discuss the three Fs and one D he got on his report card. When he told me they were eating, I said, "Okay, I'll talk to you after you eat. Have Daddy call me when you guys are done." No one ever called me back, and they didn't answer when I called them.

Throughout the night I kept thinking that one of them would call me back. When they didn't, I started to feel rejected and unloved. They must not have understood that Craig's grades were one of my biggest concerns and one of the biggest worries I had about staying in Hollywood for treatments. My worst nightmare about leaving him were coming true. Logically, I knew that there wasn't anything I could do from there because I couldn't monitor his homework, but I sure could do something when I got home. I made a vow to see to it that Craig would start turning in his work once I got home. As far as Johnny not calling back, I didn't know what to think. The last few times we had talked on the phone he seemed very distracted and eager to hang up.

A week went by before I got a call from Johnny. My phone didn't ring once, and there were no messages either. When I tried to call Johnny and Craig's phones, no one answered. Reluctantly, I decided to stop calling. For the first time since being in my little apartment, I felt lonely.

Just in time to lift my spirits I received a box full of scrapbooking supplies for the "pink" scrapbook I was planning on creating. I had told Peggy my plan when we spoke on the phone, and the next thing I knew there was a whole box of goodies waiting for me when I came back from my daily dose of radiation. Peggy and I enjoyed many long phone conversations while I was in Hollywood. Even though there is a three-hour time difference between California and Florida, being a night owl, she would talk to me for hours. There probably wasn't a topic we didn't cover at some point. The same day that Peggy's gift arrived, I received the sweetest card from my coworkers at the County. They all signed and said the kindest things about looking forward to my return. Thank God for putting those people in my life and putting me in their hearts just when I needed it most.

Trying to stay positive and think about good things and not dwell on the situation at home, I prayed that night, *Please, God, let this not turn ugly near the end. It's almost over, and I still need to keep focused on you and your peace that passes understanding.* I still didn't understand why Johnny and Craig weren't calling me.

Since my chest continued to deepen in color and become more sensitive, I decided to fill the prescription for hydrocortisone. I was shocked that a small tube about the size of a travel-size toothpaste was $45.99. I decided that since I only had another week to go I would just have to wait; I could get by using something a little less expensive.

Johnny finally called. After a chilly few minutes of conversation, I asked him what was going on and why he hadn't called me in over a week. He disclosed that he was mad because I told him to feed Craig protein.

I responded, "Are you kidding me? Because I'm concerned about my son's diet you 'punish' me for over a week?"

He said, "I know. It was dumb, but I just didn't want to hear you say anything more about it and how I was handling things while you were gone. It makes me feel like I can't do anything right. Even though you are not here, you are still trying to control everything. I'm sorry, but that's why I didn't call you or answer your phone calls."

I was stunned. I couldn't believe that he had just said that. In the past when we had arguments it would typically be over money or Craig's homework. But they were usually short-lived spats and didn't amount to much. Certainly after a couple of days we would move on. Here I was, going through one of the toughest times of my life, and he was dragging out an argument over *protein* for over a week.

Because I was so hurt by what he had just said, I responded, "Obviously you are doing fine without me, and as a matter of fact, I am doing fine without you." He sat in shocked silence for a moment and then said, "I'm sorry you feel that way," and then hung up.

Needless to say, it was a long night for me. I tossed and turned, cried in my pillow, and finally sat up in bed and wrote in my journal. It was a disgrace that under the circumstances we were having those kind of ridiculous dialogues. In my heart I knew that it would blow over, but at the time I was dejected and annoyed. It wasn't all his fault, and I knew it. I recognized after time that cancer was mainly to blame; it was taking a toll on every area of my life.

Meanwhile, my radiation rash seemed to be responding fairly well to the new cortisone cream. Generously, the nurse offered me a small sample of the otherwise cost-prohibitive medication. She only had one left but said that I could have it when I told her I really couldn't afford to pay for it at the pharmacy. Just as predicted, my chest was extremely itchy and intensely deep red, as ugly as it was uncomfortable. It is amazing how one can think nothing is wrong and before you know it things are really ugly.

February 11, 2008

I enjoyed another wonderful visit from my dear friend Renee. Although she had just taken the subway to see me a few days earlier, I was still looking forward to seeing her again. When she came up for the day, she delighted me with a walking tour of the Frank Lloyd Wright Hollyhock House. Once she discovered that it was located only a few blocks from where my apartment was, it was only a matter of planning the day before we got together and toured the charming little estate. It was always good to see Renee, but that visit was special due to the relationship pressure I was going through at the time with Johnny and Craig.

A few nights later, I was thrilled once again when Renee treated me to an evening at the Ahmanson Theater to see *The Color Purple*. When she arrived at my apartment, I asked her if she had driven her car. She said, "Of course not. I took the subway."

When I heard that I told her, "In that case, I'll drive."

Before I could even go get my keys she said, "Oh, we're going to take the subway to the theater. It's only a few blocks from here to the stop, and there's no reason to pay those outrageous parking fees when the subway will drop us off a block from the theater."

At first I wasn't sure I wanted to do that. Although Renee took public transportation everywhere, I didn't. She was not only familiar with the subways and buses in Los Angeles but was used to taking public transportation all over the world. Because I knew that about her and I trusted her judgment, I agreed. Now that I knew we would be walking, I grabbed a jacket and we set off on our adventure. We arrived in plenty of time to find our seats on the third row.

Renee had bought the tickets well in advance for this special treat just for me. She had always told me, "I'm not at the theater unless I can see the whites of the actors' eyes." And their eyes we did see. It was riveting and engulfed me from the first note that was sung to the minute the curtain went down. When Renee had first told me of her plan to take me to see it, I was hesitant. The last thing I needed was a total downer evening, and from what I remembered about the book, it was a very intense story. I was greatly relieved to see that it was not depressing; it was in fact so much more vibrant than the book. Such a wonderful musical, such a wonderful friend.

Deborah, one of my most outgoing, unabashed, and vocal friends, came to see me while I was still away from home. We grabbed lunch at a diner before she accompanied me to radiation. As usual, Mark was there to check me in, but this time Deborah was entertaining him with some outrageous story and had him laughing. That's Deb for you!

I took my seat in the lobby, but after a half an hour of waiting, which wasn't usual, my name still hadn't been called. Finally, I approached the desk and asked about it. Turns out I hadn't been signed in, thanks to Mark being quite smitten by Deborah's humor and forgetting to put me in the queue. Fortunately, I was immediately sent back for my daily dose.

That night I treated Deb to my standard fare: chicken fillets cooked in my George Foreman grill, steamed broccoli, and a half of a sweet potato. She has always been a light eater and had no complaints about the quality or quantity. Because of my diligent walking and conscious eating habits over the past few weeks I had lost ten pounds. It wasn't enough weight for any of my techs to hassle me about, but it was enough to inspire me to keep at it. Before too much longer I would have to go back to work, and I would have to wear something other than soft T-shirts and oversized sweatpants. Thirty pounds of extra weight was still plaguing me, and I was determined to get rid of it.

February 13, 2008

Finally a celebration with my lifelong friend Linda. We went to see *Wicked* in honor of my upcoming completion of radiation. To make the night even more special we were lucky enough to be winners of the Pantages lottery. Each night before the show started, the theater drew names for the front row. Our seats were almost dead center in the front row. We were close enough to the stage that we could see all the expressions on the actors' faces and every button on each of the magnificent costumes. Another fun night. It was so very different from *The Color Purple* but just as engaging and brilliant.

Linda and I had been friends since I was four years old, and because we had built such a close relationship, she easily said to me, "You don't need to be uncomfortable around me. If you're more comfortable not wearing your wig, don't feel you have to wear it in front of me." Since my hair had started to sprout it made my head extremely itchy when I put my wig on; therefore I had been going without any wig while in my apartment. Not wanting to get a sunburned head I would wear a ball cap while on my walks. Because I didn't think the ball cap was appropriate for our night at the theater, I decided to go out that night without any head covering. After that night I took several more public outings without any wig or hat. I felt I had been liberated from having to "cover the cancer."

My left side was now completely burned and was unbelievably itchy and unpleasant. Even under my arm the skin was red and swollen. Just like a massive sunburn it had started to bubble and peel. Unable to lie on my left side at night, I struggled to find a position comfortable enough to allow me to fall asleep each night. After the third week, it really started to become noticeable. Because it was almost over, they took x-rays, and that added time to my normal daily treatment. After the x-rays were studied, the treatment was recalculated. The technicians were going to concentrate on a smaller area for the last three treatments. Amusingly, the technician said to me as I was being taken off the table, "I'd say you are well done."

I replied, "Yep, I'm ready to vacate the rotisserie now."

February 14, 2008

Valentine's night I finally received a call from Johnny but not Craig. My feelings were so hurt, but I realized that I couldn't always be the center of everyone's attention. I suppose my friends had spoiled me a bit, but what I really wanted was that attention from my family. The next day was my last day of radiation, and I almost wish it wasn't. During my time in LA I had walked over seventy-five miles, lost a total of fourteen pounds, and completed thirty-six doses of radiation. Despite everything going on with my husband and son, I had stayed positive, disciplined, and mindful of my purpose in being there. That alone gave me hope for continued progress once I returned home. I prayed that my burned chest would heal enough to perhaps consider reconstruction later that year. But as I had learned nothing is a given when it comes to cancer; surprises, good luck, and bad luck lurk around every corner. It was going to be a huge transition for me to get used to working again, managing our home, and overseeing my teenage son. Soon my time would be spent coping with all of that instead of having all the time for myself. My radiation vacation was over.

> "And it came to pass at the end of forty days, that Noah opened the window of the ark which he had made" (Genesis 8:6 NKJV).

Chapter 25

BACK TO THE REAL WORLD

February 15, 2008

As we had previously agreed, Johnny showed up with his beloved truck to help me pack up my belongings and get me home. After we loaded his truck, I turned in my key and said good-bye to my Hollywood hideout. Deciding to avoid the rush-hour traffic, we drove together in his truck to a nice restaurant. That was the first dinner we had together in almost two months. During dinner I didn't want to start an argument or bring up bad feelings, so I kept my comments light. Johnny, who was by nature nonconfrontational, certainly didn't bring anything up either. I decided then that I would have to let some things go and just move forward with our "new" life together. I wanted to have a positive experience, and rehashing things wouldn't change either of us but would only stir up bad feelings. After dinner we drove back to the apartment and got my car, and we made our way back to Orange County.

As I stepped through the door of my living room, I was expecting to see a mess. Instead I was met with a tidy living room, and through the opening I saw a fairly clean kitchen. Only Craig's room looked like a bomb had exploded. As they say, "Two out of three ain't bad." Again I refrained from making comments but proceeded to unpack my things.

As I was in the bedroom unpacking my personal items, Tiki came in and jumped on the bed. I greeted her with the same phrase I always use when I've been apart from her: "Come see Momma!" And then I lay down next to her and let her give me kisses. She eagerly licked my face and leaned her whole six and a half pounds into my neck and face. I stroked her neck and gave her some kisses on top of her head. I thought as I patted her soft hair and let her lick my face how sweet she was and how she gave her love to me unconditionally. Why couldn't we all be more like dogs?

February 21, 2008

My first day back at work I was bowled over to be met with a welcome-back party by my coworkers. They had posters, balloons, and tons of food. It was all so welcoming, and it made the transition so much easier.

The most difficult part of being back to work was going to work without a wig or breasts. Given how itchy and hot the wig felt, I opted to just show off my "micro-pixie." Meanwhile, the left side of my chest was too burned to wear any kind of bra or prosthetics, so I just had to go without. My skin was noticeably burned and had started to smell like burned flesh. At first I didn't realize what the acrid odor was. Then after a couple of days I was horrified to realize that it was me! In addition to trying to hide the awful odor, I was also trying to wear things that didn't draw too much attention to my new "flat" figure. Not an easy feat to accomplish when everything seemed to rub or hurt my extremely sensitive skin. Since I was concerned about looking just a little more "manly" than I prefer, I made sure to wear stylish earrings and a vibrant shade of lipstick. Other than going to work, I didn't go out too much.

February 25, 2008

Being at work was enjoyable. Everyone continued to be kind and thoughtful, but I wish I could say the same for what was going on at home. Friday night I went to Craig and told him that it was time to stop playing video games and go to bed. For someone who had gotten used to not having rules—thanks to his father not being a disciplinarian—this didn't go over too well.

When I refused to let him have his way, he stomped off, but not before telling me he wished I'd died. I suppose most kids say as much to their parents at one time or another, but this cut me to the bone. Apparently, life was pretty good while I was in Los Angeles.

I tried to understand how difficult my illness was for him. Admittedly, there's something kind of nice and liberating about doing whatever you want with no one there to tell you otherwise. Heck, I had had forty days and forty nights of that. There's also something rather freeing in knowing you don't have any responsibilities. But then when someone steps in to tell you otherwise, that makes you angry. Yep, I get it. I just had to remind myself that raising a teenager was much like dealing with cancer: just get through it one day at a time.

Chapter 26

THE ROAD TO RECONSTRUCTION

March 2008

As far as reconstruction goes, I probably wouldn't be eligible for another year. The plastic surgeon had told me that when I met her before my surgery. Since it takes the skin several months to heal after radiation, I was told to make an appointment with her in several months. One thing I had learned throughout the previous nine months was to not get my hopes up. Unfortunately things changed all the time. Sometimes the things I thought were going to be horrible actually turned out to be quite bearable and the things I wasn't even concerned about were just the things to agitate me.

Over the past year I had dealt with a body that no longer looked like my own. My joints cried out in pain each time I lifted something or tried to pull something over my head. The hair on my head that did come in defied all rhyme or reason. Although it continued to grow back, it was coarse, grey, and out of control. When Sandy my stylist tried to do anything with it, we would end up in a fit of giggles, laughing over how much like doll hair it was. You know, when a little girl drags her baby doll around and the hair looks like a rat's nest? Yes, that was me. Each time I went in for a visit, she would cut it short in an effort to remove the chemically damaged shafts of hair. At one point she even bleached it out and gave me an edgy rocker-mom look! It was fun, and considering that it was nothing like my old style or texture of hair anyway, I thought, *Why not? It'll be grown out and cut off again in a matter of weeks.*

Not just my hair suffered, but my overall quality of life suffered tremendously as well. The small act of going on a bicycle ride with my husband had been hindered to the point where I was in tears by the time I had peddled to the end of the block. He didn't understand, and he would ride alongside of me and say, "Just push through it; you can do it!" He really didn't understand, and neither did I. Although I had been extremely active before cancer, I was now out of shape. More than that, though, the pain was like an ice pick being driven into my knees. I was having difficulty just stepping up on the curb when I went for walks with my neighbor Norma.

I had been taking the Tamoxafin ever since I returned home. Knowing that there were some side effects with that medication, I was prepared for a little stiffness and a few aches. Nothing prepared me for the extreme pain I felt in most of my joints. This was not what I had expected. I really wanted to get back to my life, but this medication was imprisoning me. Friends would ask when I would be able to join them in activities once again. Not knowing how I would feel, I wasn't making any commitments, and no one seemed to recognize why. Many people showed their enthusiasm when they learned that I had survived breast cancer. They would say things like "That's great! You're all done now!" What they didn't realize was that I had indeed survived, but like any battlefield where a war was fought, there was destruction and the restoration was not yet complete.

October 2008

After several months of enduring the aches and pains, and additional weight gain, I decided that I could not continue taking the Tamoxafin. My oncologist tried to switch me to another drug called Arimidex, another form of Aromatase inhibitors. AIs are taken by postmenopausal women diagnosed with early stage, positive hormone-receptive breast cancer to reduce the risk of the cancer coming back. AIs may cause side effects, including hot flashes, weight gain, and joint pain. About 25 percent of women who are prescribed AIs either don't take the medicine at all or stop taking it early because of side effects. It's designed for women who are postmenopausal and therefore don't need the estrogen blockers that Tamoxafin contains. Although I qualified for this drug since I had indeed gone through menopause during my chemo treatments, I too had a difficult time tolerating the side effects. After only a few short weeks of taking the medicine, I gained nine pounds, began walking as if I were ninety years old, and worse, I *felt* like I was ninety-five! After months of not being able to step up on a curb without excruciating pain in my knees or even lift a glass of water without sharp pains shooting through my elbows, I made the decision to quit the AIs. I also decided to not take *any* more medication.

When I told my oncologist that I would not be taking this medicine anymore, he was not upset. He told me that he realized that there were plenty of women who had made that same decision. The effects of the drug were just too much for some women to justify, and he agreed that it was questionable whether the means justified the end. I was surprised to hear him say that. He went on to tell me that if that was my final decision he would unfortunately no longer be seeing me. If I didn't need him to monitor my treatment and prescribe the drugs, then our paths would now have to part. Although I was initially shocked at his declaration, I shook his hand good-bye and thanked him for taking such good care of me. As I left his office for the last time, it struck me that perhaps the worst was behind me.

I was mistaken.

March 2009

Over a year had gone by since I'd left my little apartment in Hollywood. One very long year. What had driven me was the anticipation of seeing the plastic surgeon and discussing the options I might have for reconstruction. I had an appointment to see her and hoped to have a new plan for moving on with my life. It was awkward to always have to worry about my numerous chest scars showing as my blouse swung forward at the water cooler. Additionally, there was the uncomfortable weight of the prosthesis that never seem to fit right or not being able to shop for flattering tops because they didn't hide my concave chest. I had anxiously awaited that appointment, and it couldn't come soon enough.

Someone once told me that life was giving me a lot of lemons and that they knew me well and had no doubt that I would surely make some sweet lemonade. As much as I appreciated their sentiment, I felt like I had made plenty of lemonade for one lifetime, and personally I would be happy to never have to squeeze another lemon again. But it was not to be. I was allotted another batch.

My visit with the plastic surgeon was very brief. I suppose she had already made up her mind and realized that she was wasting her time as well as mine. To that end, she said almost as soon as she walked into to the exam room, "I know you are going to be unhappy with my news, but I can't help you." Startled to hear her so candidly drop that verbal bomb, I asked her to please explain. She told me that I was no longer eligible for implants since I had been subjected to such extensive radiation. Shocked, I said, "What do you mean? Half of Orange County has implants. Why can't I have them too?"

She responded, "Radiation many times, and in your case certainly, is the 'deal breaker.' Due to the damaged radiated skin, it would be inadvisable to give you implants." I sat in numb horror as she continued. "In the past, when a woman who has gone through radiation such as you have decides to have the surgical procedure to have expanders placed under her skin, she endures months of pain as the skin is slowly stretched, further subjects herself to numerous trips back and forth to the plastic surgeon's office for 'refills,' and then *finally* has implants inserted into the newly formed pouch, and then she is miserably disappointed to have the implant work its way through the radiated, damaged skin." As I sat there listening to her tell this horrific tale, I pictured myself at the neighbor's BBQ mortified to see my breast fall out on the patio.

This was crushing news to me. It was not what I expected to hear from her. Moreover, it was unacceptable. I asked her if there were other procedures we might consider, something that didn't involve implants. She said there was, but she didn't think I would be happy with it. It involved taking the muscles from my back and "tunneling" them through to the front of my body to create small "breasts." This is called a latissimus flap surgery, and she was right. It was not the answer I was looking for. I didn't want to trade my back muscles and have two huge visible scars down my back for two small breasts. I would need to think and pray about this.

Over the next few days, I held my own private pity party. I felt entitled to this and was not a very happy or pleasant person to be around. I realize now that I should have remembered something I said when I was first diagnosed with cancer and someone asked me, "Oh, no! Why you?" I responded, "Why not me?" It was not always easy, and

I didn't always want to be strong. But after a while I realized that I had come too far and could not give up.

I was determined to discover what my options were for reconstruction. I attended a seminar for women who have survived breast cancer and want to share their experiences with other women. I listened to a woman talk about her struggles, and after two years of trying to find the perfect reconstruction process for herself, she told us she would be flying to Texas to have a very specialized surgery. She was going to be receiving cadaver skin and tissue, and although she would be on antirejection drugs the rest of her life, she was excited to do so because the radiation had left her so few options. She encouraged me to do my own research but let me know that there was plenty of information on the Internet that would probably surprise me because, as we all know, and she winked, the doctors don't tell you everything.

Boy, was I surprised. I had no idea that cadaver donations were even available for breast reconstruction. In addition to this knowledge, I learned about a procedure called a TUG, where they use the inner thigh and transplant thigh tissue into the breast area by sewing the vessels together and creating a new breast, albeit a very small breast, because most thighs do not afford much tissue. Mine actually would, so I gave that some serious thought!

There is the well-known procedure called a TRAM flap, where the abdominal tissue is transferred to the breast area. I did not have enough abdominal tissue, so this was not an option my plastic surgeon had even offered me. I continued my research. I was beginning to realize that there were other options besides the latissimus flap that my plastic surgeon had originally told me was my only option. It's actually a rather archaic procedure but is still widely used and many times the only option offered. Unfortunately many women don't realize that they have other options. It takes a dedicated researcher and an aggressive approach to finding the best procedure, not just what is being offered.

Because I had discovered a variety of other procedures, I decided to get a second opinion from my plastic surgeon. Armed with an arsenal of information, I went back in anticipating that this second plastic surgeon would be on my team and would agree to one of these procedures. Instead, in the middle of my consultation, she took a phone call and left me standing in my underwear. I fully expected her to return so that I could continue to share my newfound information. After twenty minutes, when she did not return to the room, I got dressed and left the office. Needless to say I was disappointed, and it was at this precise moment that I came to the realization that I had to get outside of my current health care provider for an objective professional opinion.

As I walked to my car, the vibrations of my cell phone interrupted my deep thoughts. It was the plastic surgeon inquiring where I was. After our brief and unproductive appointment, she agreed to give me the referral outside of the current health care provider that I so desired. If truth be told, she did this out of guilt. After three weeks went by, I still did not have that second opinion authorized. I found myself writing yet another letter to the head of the plastic surgery department expressing my disappointment and reiterating my request for this out-of-network second opinion.

August 2009

After two and a half months of waiting, my request was finally approved. I was going to see a surgeon whom I believed would be qualified to discuss my being a candidate for these latest procedures. Ironically, my appointment with him was two years to the day after my mastectomy. I was excited to meet this guy. Arriving at his office, I entered an aquarium full of beautiful people. As I chatted with the woman next to me, she enthusiastically shared with me, "We love him. He got rid of a scar on my husband's forehead, and you would never know he ever had any kind of accident. He looks fabulous!" Just as she was beginning to tell me about the accident, they called me back.

The nurse left me in the exam room and instructed me to remove all clothing except my panties and sit on the exam table. This was not something that was comfortable for me, because I had gained so much weight and had a big, red, ugly 9 x 9 red patch of radiated skin along with mastectomy scars, not to mention that the room was so cold that if I still had nipples … well, you know. Sitting there *sans* robe was a feat in and of itself. I sat shivering for at least twenty minutes.

After twenty minutes the doctor bounded in. Although I was starting to get a little upset because I was freezing, I was still so excited to meet him and hear what he had to say. My high expectations were quickly shattered. As he rolled the stool uncomfortably close to me, he introduced himself and said, "Wow, you look like a Coke can."

Shocked that he would say such a thing, I mumbled, "Yes, the chemo packed on an extra forty pounds, and I still have thirty to lose."

He snapped back at me, "Well, you're not trying hard enough." He also admonished, "If you really want to lose the weight, you need to hire a personal trainer."

I knew that I wasn't there to discuss my weight loss. I would deal with that later. I wanted to know what he had to say about my options for breast reconstruction. When I responded, "That's not why I'm here. I want to ask you questions about reconstruction," he said, "There will be time for that later, but I can't do anything for you until you lose the weight, a lot of weight. Like I said, you look like a Coke can, and I can't make you look beautiful until you lose this weight. Once you lose the weight, and I mean *all the weight you can possibly lose*, then you can come back to see me. I will make breasts out of whatever is left." At this point he rolled his stool back, jumped up, and said in a rather cavalier way, "So, when you lose your weight, come back and see me, and we'll talk."

I was mortified over what had just happened. With tear-filled eyes I made my way back down to my car, where I sat and sobbed for the next half hour. Would I allow this arrogant and insensitive man to crush my dreams in one fell swoop? Unbelievably, ten minutes of his time had deflated every hope and dream that I had had of feeling like a beautiful woman again. Since I didn't get any answers about those procedures, after about a week I decided I was not going to be undone by this egomaniac. I would continue to look for a surgeon who could work with me.

Chapter 27

THE REAL SAINTS OF NEW ORLEANS

September, 2009

After many nights of researching the web, reading everything I could get my hands on and attending conferences, I found an amazing web site: BreastCancer.org. The discussion boards were full of women discussing their experiences. I must have read over five hundred discussions about Dr. DellaCroce and his team and what they were doing for women around the world. Women were flying in from all over the country as well as from Canada, Mexico, Germany, and Brazil just to have him perform this surgery. This amazing doctor and his team were rebuilding women who had been told they were damaged goods and couldn't be rebuilt. The women were raving about this amazing place called the Center for Restorative Breast Surgery in Louisiana. As soon as I went to their website, breastcenter.com, I knew I had to get in touch with them immediately.

From their website *(Permission granted by The Breast Center for Restorative Breast Surgery)*:

> Doctors Frank DellaCroce, Scott Sullivan and Christopher Trahan of the Center for Restorative Breast Surgery (CRBS) are the pioneers of a groundbreaking new breast reconstruction option. See more at:

http://www.breastcenter.com/breast-reconstruction-procedures/body-lift-flap/#sthash.YDPA8YwS.dpuf

Many people may think that reconstruction is purely cosmetic. It's not. It goes beyond what people see on the outside. I have known all along that I am much more than my breasts. I am intelligent, witty, loving, kind, and spirit-filled. I am also a woman who enjoys looking feminine and feeling confident in my clothes as well as my own skin. The AMA says this about reconstruction: postmastectomy reconstruction in a breast cancer patient is not "cosmetic surgery." The American Medical Association makes a distinction between "cosmetic surgery" and "reconstructive surgery" in its policy compendium (American Medical Association, House of Delegates. AMA Policy Compendium. Chicago, IL, H-475.992:616, 1989).

The AMA policy says this:

> H-475.992 Definitions of "Cosmetic" and "Reconstructive" Surgery—(1) The AMA supports the following definitions of "cosmetic" and "reconstructive" surgery: Cosmetic surgery is performed to reshape normal structure of the body in order to improve the patient's appearance and self-esteem. Reconstructive surgery is performed on abnormal structures of the body caused by congenital defects, developmental abnormalities, trauma, infection, tumors or disease. It is generally performed to improve function, but may also be done to approximate a normal appearance. (2) The AMA encourages third-party payers to use these definitions in determining services eligible for coverage under the plans they offer or administer.

By extension, if a surgical procedure is classified as "reconstructive," it is considered medically necessary, while "cosmetic surgery" is not. Third-party payers not only use those definitions when considering payment for medical services, but coverage of reconstruction during the course of breast cancer treatment is mandated by federal law in the United States. It is not "cosmetic surgery."

January 2010

I made all of the important changes necessary in regards to my health insurance. I left my previous carrier and joined a PPO. I did this so that some of the fee would be covered by insurance, although I was responsible for a large amount of the cost of this surgery. I was told that these doctors believed so strongly in what they were doing for women that they would find a way to make it all work for me.

I sent them pictures, and they agreed that I was a suitable candidate. When I wrote to the doctor and asked him if I was too fat, his response was music to my ears. He wrote back, "No, you are perfect." I bought the plane tickets for Cathy and me to travel to New Orleans and then found out later that the American Cancer Society will provide airfare for a cancer patient and their caregiver to fly if it's necessary for a medical procedure. Unfortunately, they would not reimburse—another reason that it's good to research as much as you can. I was so preoccupied with gathering information about the facility and the procedure that I neglected to check out things like that. However, I would leave for the Big Easy in a few weeks, and I had plenty of other things to work on, so I couldn't worry about something that was already done. Additionally, I would be out of work for another six weeks after I returned from the surgery.

It seemed like so much to go through, but I continued to be motivated by 2 Timothy where we are told that we have been given a spirit of power and love and self-discipline. It definitely took some self-discipline to continue to research and make arrangements. All of these duties fell to me now that my dear friend Laura was having her own health issues. She had been such an advocate for me, even going so far as to read my insurance plan and help me look at a budget for things my insurance would not cover. I missed her diligent support but knew that this was not the time for me to ask for her help. Although I was still able to talk with her and keep her informed about the upcoming reconstruction, I tried to focus on our friendship and things she might be needing rather than me and my issues.

Although Johnny had told me to do whatever I felt I needed to do in order to feel whole again, I did not expect him to assist in the planning of it. Johnny wasn't a planner; he preferred to be spontaneous with his life. As luck would have it, I was a planner, and the task at hand was going to require discipline and effort to make sure all the pieces lined up. There were issues regarding the aftercare I would have to prepare for as well as the time I would be gone. Craig would need a more scheduled approach to doing his homework and getting the help he might need for tests. Luckily, I wouldn't be gone much more than two weeks, but the recovery time would be substantial. I would not be able to lift, drive, clean, cook, or do laundry for a while. After I recovered from the initial surgery, I would need to fly back to New Orleans and have part two of my extensive reconstruction. There were so many things to plan for; I needed to get to work.

March 2010

Three days after Mardi Gras and a couple of weeks after Drew Brees led the New Orleans Saints to a victory, I walked into Dr. DellaCroce's office at the Center for Restorative Breast Surgery in New Orleans and felt an immediate sense of comfort. The spa-like setting, the daylight streaming in from the vaulted glass ceiling, and the professional demeanor of the staff all contributed to my overall feeling of serenity. Dr. DellaCroce was adorable. With his delightfully soft southern accent (think Mathew McConaughey), he proceeded to explain the entire process of the GAP reconstruction. It didn't matter that I had already done quite a bit of research on my own. Cathy and I listened with rapt attention as he gave us even more understanding of this highly complex surgery. He explained that this surgery was for women with otherwise inadequate tummy tissue; miraculously the breast may be reconstructed with tissue borrowed from the gluteal area. Skin, fat, and the tiny feeding blood vessels are collected without loss of underlying muscle tissue. Amazingly, the fatty tissue is removed from the excess in the upper hip, providing a closure line that would be concealed under normal underwear. Realizing that I wasn't going to be overly endowed (I had never had big hips or bottom), at the same time I was overjoyed at relocating some unwanted fat. What woman wouldn't be? I can't tell you how many women offered to donate theirs when I told them about this surgery.

Dr. DellaCroce went on to say that perforator flaps (as they are called) represent the state of the art in breast reconstruction. Replacing the skin and soft tissue removed at mastectomy with soft, warm, living tissue is accomplished by borrowing skin and fatty tissue from the abdomen or hip. All this is accomplished without sacrificing muscles and strength as compared to less-sophisticated techniques. At this point I realized that this was a whole different league. What had previously been so flippantly offered to me as my "only choice" was kindergarten compared to what this man was offering. And what about the egomaniac who had told me I looked like a Coke can? I couldn't restrain myself, and I told Dr. DellaCroce about what the other surgeon had said to me. He was shocked and sad for me. "Not to worry," he told me. From here on out it would be about what I wanted and how I felt. Finally.

After my consultation with the doctor I was taken into another room for photos to be taken. Once again I admired how they seemed to pay attention to every detail; thoughtfully there was a warm heater perched on a stand in the front of the room where I was to stand while posing for my before shots! After the first sets of photos were taken I donned a robe and returned to Dr. DellaCroce, who proceeded to mark my body with a blue marker. Then back in for what I like to call my blue-period photo shoot. After I dressed I was given a packet of information and a pair of luxurious spa socks for my stay in the hospital. Yes, they thought of everything.

The night before a surgery is typically filled with anxiety, apprehension, and concern. Not this one. I can honestly say that all I felt was anticipation and confidence. After having done extensive research and then meeting my completely qualified surgeon, I was actually eager to get this show on the road! Since I was allowed to eat up until midnight, Cathy and I walked down to the French Quarter and found a wonderful outdoor café serving fresh-out-of-the-fryer beignets and steaming hot chocolate. We sat under the heat lamps and listened to a local musician named Steamboat Willy and thoroughly enjoyed the cool March evening. We marveled at how forty years ago when we first met as children at church it would have never entered our minds that someday we would be sitting in New Orleans eating beignets while awaiting the *Graff Pink Diamond* equivalent of surgical breast reconstruction.

The next morning in true rock star fashion there was a limousine waiting to take me to the hospital. What a relief to not have to worry about any of those necessary details. They took care of getting us to and from our hotel and hospital as well as back to the airport when needed. The limo driver was especially gentle and gracious. He treated me like a fragile princess. After I arrived at the hospital, I was fitted with the latest in hospital fashion: a gown, a hairnet, and an IV. When I was snug in my gurney, Cathy came to my side, brushed my hair up under my cap, and then prayed over me. Right before going into the operating room, Dr. DellaCroce came in to see me. He wanted to make sure the markings he had made on me the day before had not worn off. He smiled his cute smile, asked me if I was ready to rock and roll, and winked. The nurses came to get me, we began to roll, and then I was out.

Waking up in the ICU after the surgery the first thing I remember was the feeling of unbearable heat! I asked the nurse for a cold compress, and as soon as it was placed on my head it was hot. It is my understanding that it was the anesthesia and many women are affected in this way. It took a couple of days for the anesthesia to wear off, not surprising since I was in surgery for almost ten hours. Upon waking I also discovered a pain management "ball" attached by tubes to my surgical sites along the hipline where the tissue had been removed. This ball was full of a Novocain-type medicine steadily allowing the area to be numb so that I could comfortably lie in the bed. Additionally, I had a series of wires connected to a Doppler device monitoring the new breasts. My body was encased in a black body garment from the knees up to the waist that applied pressure to the site and kept things locked in place. There were drains coming out of four sites with little bulbs of fluid at the end. I looked like something out of a Frankenstein movie, but in a more delicate way!

Over the next twenty-four hours the blood supply to the new breasts was constantly monitored as I fell in and out of sleep. The pain was really not too bad; the drugs took care of that. It wasn't until I was ready to sit up for the first time that I felt the force of what my body had just been through. As I swung my legs over the side of the bed I felt a "whoosh" of blood going to my chest and I immediately felt sick to my stomach. Part of what I was experiencing was the remainder of anesthesia in my system. As I threw up, I saw a lot of black gunk that I knew I certainly didn't want in my body anymore. Afterward I felt much better.

Over the next few days I would need to have the drains carefully measured and emptied, along with keeping an eye on the new breasts.

They were carefully bandaged, but now I had to pay attention to how they felt; ideally, they should be warm to the touch. After the first seventy-two hours, the Doppler was removed and I needed to monitor them myself; this was made clear to me given that there was no longer any sensation in them, and I knew there never would be. Another part of my life stolen by cancer.

Once I was released from the hospital I was taken (by limousine) back to my hotel. My research had led me to the Hilton Hotel near the French Quarter. They were close enough to the breast center to make it convenient for Cathy but also close to the center of activities so that within walking distance there would always be something interesting to see or do. The Hilton also provided a breakfast and light dinner for anyone staying with them. This was an added bonus since my caregiver-friend Cathy would be able to eat there and not have to walk by herself to get dinner. After dinner each night, Cathy called or e-mailed Johnny to let him know how I was doing. She also went online to inform a group of former breast center patients (my newfound friends) of my recovery process.

Cathy was tasked with the challenge of monitoring the four drains I had protruding from my body as well as dispensing the pain meds. She had to empty the drains and record all fluids that came out. As only a true friend can do, she did it gently and patiently. She was such a good nurse that ten days after surgery Cathy suggested that we walk over to the French Quarter. Although I was taking pain pills and this was still quite a feat for me, I agreed. How could I be in New Orleans and not spend a little more time in the French Quarter? As I gathered up my four drains, slid my feet into sandals, and stepped onto the elevator, I felt like I was lugging an extra twenty-five pounds of weight. Disappointingly, it wasn't all breast!

Cathy and I set out at 10:00 in the morning to go explore the French Quarter. Every hour or so we would find a place for me to sit and rest. Cathy was good about asking people to help provide a resting spot. However, at one point she needed to excuse herself to go to the rest room, and she left me looking around in the shop next door. The proprietor came out and said, "Good morning. How are you today?"

I answered, "Good morning. I'm okay." I evidently spoke a bit too weakly for her taste.

She quickly snapped back, "What do you mean okay? Just okay?"

At first I smiled, and then in my drug-induced reasoning I began to get feisty. Since Cathy wasn't there to stop me I countered, "Well, I just got out of the hospital after a ten-hour surgery, and today is my first day out walking. I'm still carrying drains, and I'm starting to get a little tired. So for me, okay is actually pretty darned good!"

As I said this I lifted my shirt just enough for her to see the engorged hand grenades of body fluid. We had been out for the past five hours! Her mouth dropped open, her eyes bulged, and she stammered, "Why, uh, oh goodness. Well, uh, you take care of yourself."

Just as she was saying that Cathy walked in and saw the look on the shopkeeper's face. Cathy turned a suspicious eye on me and asked what was going on and if was I okay. I said, "I'm fine. I was just feeling a bit winded and in need of a resting spot. I think we need to go sit down somewhere."

Later, as we sat under a shady tree sipping some iced tea, I told her the whole story. She scolded me, but she was laughing as she did so. Cathy quipped, "She's lucky you didn't also show her the ten-inch incisions. She might have passed out." It's fortunate that Cathy came back when she did or I might have done just that.

By the time two weeks had passed, I was allowed to travel back home. Cathy and I checked out of the hotel, and the limousine from the breast center arrived to take us to the airport. When we arrived at the airport, the driver retrieved a wheelchair for me. As I sat in the wheelchair waiting for the curbside porter to check my bags, I marveled at what a difference two weeks had made. My thoughts were suddenly interrupted as I realized that Cathy was unpacking her suitcase right there on the sidewalk. It was several pounds over the weight limit, and she needed to unload some items. Turns out she had purchased a case of water to have in the hotel room. When we hadn't consumed it all, she had packed the remainder! Once she got rid of her "water weight" she was within the weight limit and we were free to move on into the airport.

We now had to pass through airport security. Although I was allowed to remain in the wheelchair, they still passed the wand over me. At once the TSA agent was alarmed; she had discovered my "grenades." Her eyes were wide as she instructed me to "stand up!" I quickly realized what was happening and quickly shoved my letter of explanation in her face as I said, "I just had surgery, and this will explain it." After reading it, she resumed her professional demeanor and kindly allowed me to roll on through the checkpoint. I was smart enough to not say anything to Cathy until we were well out of earshot, at which point she immediately burst out laughing.

Knowing that I would probably need a break after the confines of the airplane, we had arranged for a two-hour break in Denver. We were able to have dinner before changing planes. The Denver airport has a service that will pick you up at the gate and take you via an electric cart to your next gate. In our case our friendly driver took us to a restaurant and told us to flag him down again when we were ready to go to our departure gate. After our meal I made my way to the restroom. When I returned I found my dear friend in tears. She composed herself enough to share with me that upon calling home she had learned that her own father had been rushed to the hospital and was not expected to live. I felt horrible for her. I also felt a ton of guilt. She had put her own life on hold in order to accompany me on this two-week medical adventure. She had been patient, giving, and understanding in ways most people never could have been. She thoughtfully allowed my husband to stay home with our son while she was with me, changing bulbs of body fluid. Being friends since we were ten years old meant crossing a lot of bridges; this was certainly one of our most challenging.

I don't even remember how we got ourselves to the gate or when we departed. I do know that by the time we touched down at John Wayne Airport in Orange County we were both exhausted and ready for Johnny to pick us up. What a surprise to find him and my son there … in the truck! Not the truck again! Was this my husband's go-to vehicle when his wife was full of drains and could barely move? There must have been something comforting about this vehicle, something that told him it was all going to be all right. Why else would he have driven that thing each time he picked me up from a major surgery? My son must have been reading my mind, because he whispered to me, "Sorry, Mom. Let me help you up." What a day.

After measuring body fluids, I was faced with the task of trying to peel the compression garment off for a shower and then having Johnny assist in pouring my swollen body back into the unforgiving girdle-like suit. It was virtually impossible to negotiate this garment on my own. It was a circuitous effort of maneuvering and then zipping, on both sides from knee to rib cage, the series of hook-and-eye closures, all while ensuring that the tubes and drain bulbs would drain properly and remain kink free.

A compression garment holds everything locked and loaded from where the tissue has been removed and painstakingly relocated. I had two ten-inch scars across my hips in addition to all of the scarring that comes from the tissue transplant of the breasts. I didn't have any feeling in my breasts; instead there was a lot of numbness around the surgical areas as they were healing. I didn't realize it then, but I would never have any feeling in my hip area again.

Once again, the fluids needed to be drained and measured and everything recorded until the fluid reached less than twenty cc. Once the fluid measured less than twenty cc and remained there for three days, I was informed that the tube and drain could be removed. Even though I could have asked a local plastic surgeon to remove the tubes for me, I opted to have my more-than-willing husband pull the tubes out. Johnny is not at all squeamish. Truthfully, I suspect he actually enjoyed it. Miraculously, it wasn't painful. It was just kind of a creepy feeling, like when one accidentally almost swallows a long hair and is able to retrieve that piece before it completes the journey down the throat.

I was preparing myself for the pain that I felt when the drainage tubes came out after my double mastectomy. That had been excruciating. There had been some suction involved and it was actually sucking on a nerve in my chest. It had felt like an ice pick was being shoved into my chest, and I was expecting that type of pain. Much to my delight, it did not hurt at all, perhaps because I was actually numb this time. And when the tube finally popped out past the incision, it was more of a relief than anything.

In all I had four drains, one on each hip and one under each arm. The drains were rather unsightly, as they hung out underneath my baggy clothes. On days when it was necessary for me to be more compact I donned one of my trusty camisoles with the built-in pockets in which I could tuck my drains. That and baggy sweats to hide the compression garment and all of its extra bulk became my new standard wardrobe. Not too long after returning home I was able to get rid of two of the drains. The last two "hung around" for a while.

Drains were not my only issue. I had stitches next to where the drains came out of my hips, and I had glue all over the new breasts and upper hip area. The cutting-edge procedure is to glue patients back together, not stitch them. To that end, I had very ugly black cut lines from where the blood had mixed in with the purple glue that they had used to glue me back together, so I was looking like Ms. Shelley's famous character. The glue eventually began to peel off around six weeks after returning home, and I could see the actual scars underneath.

During this awkward time my friends tried to lift my spirits and give me something to look forward to. Renee, who had already sat through chemo with me, and had taken me to see *The Color Purple,* put together what she thought would be a really fun night. She decided that we would go to the theater again, in downtown LA. What she neglected to tell me is that we were going to have to walk and that there would be some hiking involved. She, being the one to always locate a deal, found us discount parking seven blocks away from the theater, and we're talking downtown Los Angeles's big city blocks, including steep hills. So we parked and set out for the theater. I was so excited to be out of the house and enjoying the theater again that I wasn't really thinking about how far we were walking, until three blocks into it my garment started to creep down my legs and tug on my dangling appendages. She was moving on ahead of me. She was marching on. Glancing back, she noticed that I was falling behind and said, "Come on. We're going to miss curtain time. Come on! We've got fifteen minutes until curtain."

I thought, *Oh no. I'd better pick up the pace.* But I was beginning to huff and puff. It was a lot of climbing, and the more I climbed the steep hills of downtown Los Angeles in a skin tight girdle, the more I fell behind. It was a lot more difficult climbing the hills of Los Angeles in a compression garment and appropriate theater clothes than I thought it would be. I think Renee finally realized that I was taking a little longer than I used to and slowed down a bit, but she continued to remind me that we had to keep on going or we would not get to our seats in time. The show was fabulous, and the walk home was much easier. It was downhill.

I should explain about wearing the garment: One must wear it twenty-four/seven, and when nature calls, there is an opening for you to go to the bathroom without removing the garment. That being said, you must wear loose pants over the garment. Well, I got so used to wearing the garment and sitting on the toilet with the garment on that a couple of times I forgot to pull my pants down and sat on the toilet to go to the bathroom and flooded my pants.

The other issue is that because your rear end is numb, you don't always feel if your pants are falling down. Once I didn't tighten my sweat pants enough, and they started coming down. Although I had the garment on underneath, it was still pretty unsightly to see. Imagine someone walking with their pants hanging down and having their butt exposed. Did you know I started that look? Those rappers ain't got nothing on me. It wasn't until I noticed that my walking was being impaired that I noticed what was happening. I couldn't wait to get rid of that garment.

By the time I was finally able to remove the drains and rid myself of the garments, it was time to get back on the airplane and head back to New Orleans for part two—a six-hour surgery and the final steps necessary in completing my reconstruction. This time Johnny went with me; he was able to set aside time from his projects at his shop to join me. My parents made arrangements to come to our house and stay with Craig. My mom is a great cook and they both adored Craig, so it was a mutually agreeable situation. Besides, this trip would require less time recuperating in the hospital and a briefer stay in New Orleans. Even after I left the hospital, I stayed in the hotel room sleeping for two days while Johnny hopped on a trolley and went off to discover the epicurean delights that the French Quarter had to offer. Shortly after I awoke from my sleep, he returned with a beignet, a po' boy, and a beautiful bracelet that I had admired in a gift shop the night before my surgery.

On the third day I went to get my new breasts tattooed. When I arrived for the consultation with the tattoo artist, he asked me what I would like: traditional areolas? If so, what color would I like? He produced a whole palette of shades for me to choose from ranging from the palest of tans to the darkest of maroon. Perhaps I would like small flowers?

I beamed and said, "I had no idea I had a choice!" In an instant I knew what I wanted; I was going to get the special tattoos that the radiation tattoo artist had not given me. Johnny thought that this was a terrific solution for the California girl who had lost her breasts. Dr. DellaCroce had inspired me to "go for it" when he told me about his belief that women were God's greatest gift. After I thought about that, I decided that I could never recreate what God had given me, but with the help of Dr. DellaCroce, I could be very happy with what I now had. When I returned home from New Orleans a week later, I still had two drains swinging from my hips, but I also sported two new seashells. If you are ever on the beach in the south of France and you see a women showing off her seashells, it may just be me.

The next day I felt a little better and well enough to walk a block as I was being encouraged to walk anyway with the new drains in place, so we experienced a lovely dinner our last night in the Big Easy.

Finally I went home, again wearing a full body-compression garment, but this time I was given a compression garment that went up and over my shoulders to keep it from sliding down since I had expressed my frustration over the last garment's reaction to the effects of gravity.

I was now wearing my new and improved body-compression garment with over-the-shoulder suspension in case I had the opportunity to once again go on a vigorous hike on my way to a Broadway show sporting an overlay of theater attire with my friend Renee. And most certainly she would be calling.

This time it was another nine weeks of drains. For some reason, they just didn't want to quit draining. My body kept pumping out that healing fluid, and I kept having to measure and dispose of body fluids. Although the fluids had become clear in color, not the original reddish color, due to postsurgical blood mixed in with the fluid, I still was putting out ninety cc a day. This startled me as my body should not still be producing this much healing fluid. I called Dr. DellaCroce's office and asked for instructions. It was a relief when I was told to go ahead and remove the drains. Hallelujah.

Now I was free. With the drains removed and the compression garment soon to be discarded for the last time, I was excited to begin my new life. Although I never felt defined by my breasts, it definitely was a struggle to dress my new body and work around something that I had had since I was twelve years old. I finally felt more like the Tammy before cancer. After I had been home a few months, one of my friends asked me if it wasn't about time for me to get a new car. I looked at her and without missing a beat said, "Nope. I just purchased new headlights."

Chapter 28

THE NEW ME

January 2011

The rest of 2010 was spent recovering from the most extensive surgeries I had ever endured. It was a long time before I was ready to exercise or even think about getting back in shape. To think that I had been so focused on my weight, and after the two reconstruction surgeries, all I wanted was to feel "normal" again. That feeling came by Christmas of 2010.

By January I was ready to commit to a whole new way of living my life. The first big change came with the new exercise program I started. Although I had always been a power walker, I hadn't seen any weight-loss benefits, just enhanced stamina. In addition to being able to power walk six miles, I had an interesting conversation with an x-ray technician. When I went in for a follow-up chest x-ray, the technician came out to the small waiting area and with a look of shock on his face said, "I'm sorry, but I have to retake the x-rays. Are you an athlete or something?"

I laughed, thinking to myself that he obviously must have me confused with some other patient, and said, "Far from it, but I have been a power walker for years. Does that count? Why are you asking?"

He responded rather sheepishly, "I just looked at your x-rays. Your lungs were too long and didn't fit on the film. I typically only see that in athletes. Very unusual, especially since you are so short it should not have been a problem." Pleased with that knowledge I followed him back into the x-ray room, where he took the second set of pictures and again expressed his amazement. Five foot one and all lungs.

My new exercise program was a major step up from power walking. My son had received P90-X for Christmas. It was one of the most intense workouts on the market at the time. He was on the water polo team at his high school and needed to get into better shape. P90-X promised to provide not only stamina but strength training too for anyone who could keep up.

Craig said, "Come on, Mom. You keep saying you want to lose the chemo weight; now is the time."

Besides the truth of that statement I also saw this as a great way to do something positive with my son. It had been a long three years. The majority of our focus as a family had been about cancer, and now we could do something positive together to turn the tide. I agreed, and right after the new year began, we started P90X. Six days a week for the required thirteen weeks we let Tom Horton guide our afternoon workout and guide us toward the promised results. We kicked, punched, jumped, squatted, lunged, and yoga'd our way toward fitness. Well, sort of. My stamina was improved, my flexibility increased, and my endorphins were raised. Unfortunately, I only lost eight pounds. Meanwhile my sixteen-year-old son was looking like a model—not fair!

At the end of thirteen weeks I was ready for a break, but I didn't want to give up on the hope of losing the weight. I went back to my computer to do more research. It wasn't long before I realized that exercise alone was not going to do it; I was going to have to make major changes in my diet. This surprised me, since I was already a very healthy eater. I was not an overeater and would enjoy desserts only so often. I looked for healthy treats and would usually order a salad for my lunch if I went out with friends. My routine was to eat very little breakfast, perhaps a protein shake if I needed a boost before an especially active day. I learned through my research that there were too many unforgiving substances in those protein shakes, too much sugar and not enough solid fuel for my body to perform as it should. Unbeknownst to me, I was doing it all wrong, and many of the actual food choices I was making were the reason I could not lose any weight. After many months of research I decided that I would go for this radical innovative way of eating and see what happened.

Willing to make big changes, I began by cleaning out all of my kitchen cupboards. This was necessary if we were to start fresh. Sugar was the first thing to go. In my readings, I discovered the evils of the white substance. Simply put, sugar creates inflammation in the body, and inflammation inhibits the body's ability to fight disease. The inability to fight disease in my body meant that I was leaving myself open for another bought of cancer. My doctor had in fact told me, "Once the door to cancer has been opened, you are never really safe. You must be vigilant in staying healthy and being aware of choices you make in the future." His voice came ringing back to me, and I realized that sugar was not only making me fat but could be killing me as well.

A few months after starting my new regime I spoke to another very beautiful female doctor and shared my philosophy with her. She looked at me with the most beautiful clear eyes and the creamiest, smoothest skin I'd ever seen on an adult (that wasn't cosmetically enhanced) and said, "I wouldn't touch it [sugar] with a ten-foot pole. It is poison, and it is as addictive as cocaine."

Eliminating sugar is indeed very difficult to do. Not only is it in almost everything that is prepackaged, but it is highly addictive. It takes a good three weeks to really stop craving sugar. Once I made it through that time period I was flourishing. As luck would have it, during that same period of time, Johnny was diagnosed with early stages of diabetes. He was immediately put on a medication called Metformin to help control his blood sugar levels. Additionally, his doctor urged him to radically change his diet. This being the case, I declared that the whole family would be "sugar free," at least in the home.

At first my son was not so sure about the new dietary adjustment. After all, cereal, cookies, all the snacks he had grown up with, and his favorite, ketchup, were suddenly taboo. I told him, "I can't control what you eat with your friends, but at least be aware of the choices you are making."

I didn't just eliminate sugar-laden desserts, but I read every single label before I put it in to my grocery cart. Not only were we sugar free; we were not eating artificial sweeteners either. Now I love a good dessert, so that brought me back to my research. As a result I learned of the magic of stevia, a natural plant that is actually sweeter than sugar with *no calories*! Hallelujah! I quickly learned to make brownies, fudge, and even root beer with stevia. I realized that I *could* have my cake and eat it too.

Since I had eliminated sugar, I felt that I needed to eliminate the things that turned to sugar once they entered the body. No more rice, potatoes, or bread. I started using coconut and other nut-based flours to make my goodies. I started making all of my own salad dressing by combining coconut oil, stevia, and spices. Not only did I love it, but Johnny and Craig did too.

It wasn't too long after we made the necessary dietary adjustments that we all noticed extreme changes in our bodies. First and most importantly, my husband's doctor looked at him a few short months later in shock and said, "Unbelievable! What have you done? Whatever it is, it is working, and you have completely reversed the diabetes! There is no need for you to continue on the medication and obviously no need for the insulin injections I had planned to discuss today."

Needless to say, my husband was then a convert too. Something else amazing happened after that: he became nice again. That sounds odd to say, but he was under so much stress with my illness, eating way more than he needed to and ultimately feeling miserable because of it. With the healthy reversal of diabetes, he not only lost thirty-five pounds but regained his playful personality. He felt better on the inside and looked better on the outside. It was a complete win-win for him.

Over the past three years, my own thirty-five pounds of chemo weight had been my only concern when it came to losing weight. It had never occurred to me that he had thirty-five pounds to lose too! He certainly started looking better, and most of his friends commented on how much younger he looked. In addition to the visual transformation that I could clearly see, an emotional shift took place as well. Johnny melted my heart one night when he said, "I'd like to think the worst is behind us and now we can begin to fall in love with each other again." There were some things cancer could not steal from me.

My own journey that year resulted in the loss of not just thirty-five pounds but an additional five! Not only did I lose the weight, but I shifted the weight around, so I actually weighed more than I had in my teenage years and twenties but I was fitting into the same size fours that I had been wearing at that age. My son was impressed, although he wasn't completely committed to the eating plan. He did know that there would be no more sugar in our home. If he wanted to eat something from the forbidden zone, he could. I wasn't looking to be the food police. I was just committed to our family's health. It was something that had made such a huge difference that I couldn't ever go back to the old, unmindful way of eating.

Because we had all endured a lengthy battle and it had been over three years since we had taken a family vacation, we decided to plan a trip to Hawaii. It would be my five-year survivor anniversary in August 2012, and we wanted to be in a happy place for that significant occasion. My boss was delighted that I was finally going to do something fun and non-cancer-related. When I asked her about taking the time off, she said, "Go. Have a great time, and don't think about work at all! You deserve it."

Once again I found myself in front of my computer undertaking extensive research. This time the subject at hand was fun! There were numerous activities to consider: snorkeling, zip-lining, tubing through the canals, off-roading in a Jeep, swimming, hiking the waterfalls, and skydiving; I wanted to do it all! As I happily planned our family vacation to Hawaii, I couldn't help but be reminded of how blessed I truly was. I recognized that there was no way I could have gone through the three years of cancer without the support of a loving family, the amazing kindness of friends, and even the generosity of a few strangers. I also realized that God was good, good all the time.

> "So do not fear, for I am with you; do not be dismayed, for I am your God. I will strengthen you and help you; I will uphold you with my righteous right hand" (Isaiah 41:10 NIV).

Epilogue

FIVE YEARS AFTER DIAGNOSIS

Free falling from ten thousand feet doesn't feel anything like people think it will. The fear is actually right before you leave the plane: knowing what you are about to do, thinking about it but not yet doing it. That's what gets you worked up. Once you take the first step and begin the experience, there's no looking back. There is only the intense force of nature rushing up to meet your body and the undeniable thought that this had better work out. When I first went skydiving, just before we left the plane, my dive instructor leaned his face toward my ear and said, "Don't worry; you're not going anywhere that I'm not going too." With those words, I let go and began to fall.

Once I jumped out of the plane and began my free fall to earth, I began to recognize that this was the perfect conclusion to the journey I had begun five years before. Just like skydiving, there is no turning back cancer; there is only going forward. And whether it was cancer or whatever else life had in store for me, I knew that I would not be going anywhere that He would not be going too. He took my fear away and turned it into the experience of a lifetime.

Postscript

In 2013, one week after my son graduated from high school, I was laid off from my job with the County of Orange. I did not consider this as life giving me more lemons; instead, I recognized that I had just been given another opportunity to make lemonade. I finally had the time to complete my book! Lemonade, anyone?

If you enjoyed this book, found it helpful, or gave it as a gift, I'd like to know. Please leave a review on Amazon.com. If you have suggestions, I welcome your feedback; contact me at TamaraKayeSeverin.com.

Resources

BreastCancer.org: The first place you should go! Hint: community boards/discussions are a wealth of information and support.

NationalBreastCancer.org: The *other* first place you should go.

AmericanCancerSociety.org: A great resource; will pay for airline tickets for treatments out of area.

BreastCenter.com: The Center for Restorative Breast Surgery. The *real* saints of New Orleans work here!

MyBreastCancerTreatment.org: Provides much-needed information on treatment options.

ww5.komen.org: All things Susan G. Komen. My local chapter provided me with a free wig/hat/scarf.

CureToday.com: Cancer updates, research, and education.

TamaraKayeSeverin.com: Visit my website and join my blog for more inspiration and resources.

PinkRibbon.com: Informative site for all things pink. Plus, great gifts to encourage loved ones going through cancer.

NBCAM.org: National public service organizations, medical associations, and government agencies promote breast cancer awareness and share information.

TheBreastCancersite.thegreatergood.com: Information, ways to help, and shopping for all things helpful in fighting cancer.

CaringBridge.org: A great way to keep everyone updated. Websites are packed with features geared to connect everyone in your "caring community," from direct caretakers to family and friends, frequent visitors, and well-wishers from far and wide.

Healthy Choices

CoconutOil.com: Great source for research and news on the health benefits of coconut oil.

TropicalTraditions.com: My resources for purchasing all things coconut.

SteviaInfo.com: Great information on Stevia, the calorie-free, all-natural sweetener.

LittleChoicesMatter.com: A wonderful place to find a variety of healthy and sugar-free seasonings, supplements, and more!

Stevia.com: Recipes, products, and FAQs.

SugarFreeMom.com: Great recipes and treats your whole family will enjoy.

BBC-Breast Before Cancer

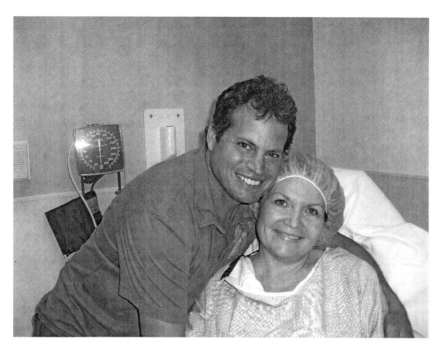

Day of Surgery

Alien for Halloween

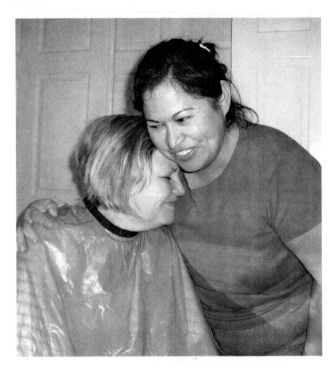

Norma Haircut

Ronna and Tiki

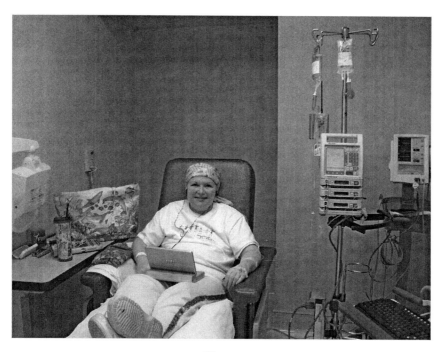

Chemo

Blonde w/Hat

Boobie Cookies

Brown wig + 30lbs.

Christmas with Laura

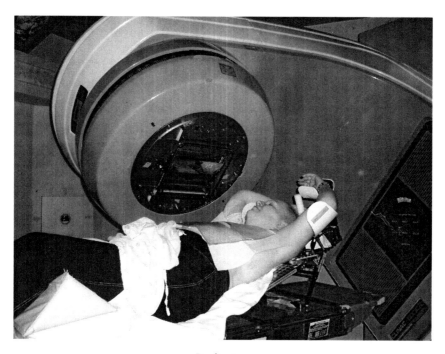

Radiation

Myself and Renee in Hollywood

New Hair

Wicked with Linda

Susan G Koman with Tiki

Hair May 2008

New white Hair

Hair Stylist Sandy

Mardi Gras

New Orleans with Cathy

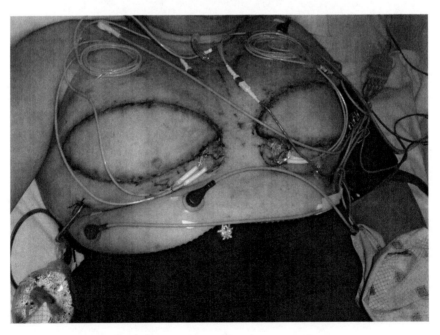

Doppler monitors after reconstruction

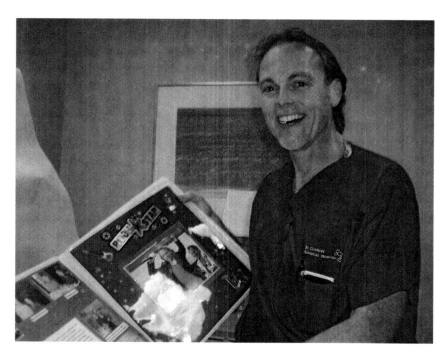

Dr. DelleCroce

Sea Shells

Celebrating 5 Year Anniversary with Laura

Sky Dive Hawaii

Tammy celebrating 5 years

CPSIA information can be obtained at www.ICGtesting.com
Printed in the USA
BVOW04s1905280614

357622BV00003B/7/P